MW01199332

It was only a matter of time before a clever publisher realized that there is an audience for whom *Exile on Main Street* or *Electric Ladyland* are as significant and worthy of study as *The Catcher in the Rye* or *Middlemarch* … The series … is freewheeling and eclectic, ranging from minute rock-geek analysis to idiosyncratic personal celebration — *The New York Times Book Review*

Ideal for the rock geek who thinks liner notes just aren't enough — *Rolling Stone*

One of the coolest publishing imprints on the planet — *Bookslut*

These are for the insane collectors out there who appreciate fantastic design, well-executed thinking, and things that make your house look cool. Each volume in this series takes a seminal album and breaks it down in startling minutiae. We love these. We are huge nerds — *Vice*

A brilliant series … each one a work of real love — *NME* (UK)

Passionate, obsessive, and smart — *Nylon*

Religious tracts for the rock 'n' roll faithful — *Boldtype*

[A] consistently excellent series — *Uncut* (UK)

We … aren't naive enough to think that we're your only source for reading about music (but if we had our way … watch out). For those of you who really like to know everything there is to know about an album, you'd do well to check out Continuum's "33 1/3" series of books — *Pitchfork*

For reviews of individual titles in the series, please visit our blog at 333sound.com and our website at http://www.bloomsbury.com/musicandsoundstudies

Follow us on Twitter: @333books

Like us on Facebook: https://www.facebook.com/33.3books

For a complete list of books in this series, see the back of this book

For more information about the series, please visit our new blog:

www.333sound.com

Where you'll find:

– Author and artist interviews

– Author profiles

– News about the series

– How to submit a proposal to our open call

– Things we find amusing

Low

Hugo Wilcken

BLOOMSBURY ACADEMIC
NEW YORK · LONDON · OXFORD · NEW DELHI · SYDNEY

BLOOMSBURY ACADEMIC
Bloomsbury Publishing Inc
1385 Broadway, New York, NY 10018, USA
50 Bedford Square, London, WC1B 3DP, UK

BLOOMSBURY, BLOOMSBURY ACADEMIC and the Diana logo are trademarks of
Bloomsbury Publishing Plc

First published in 2005 by the Continuum International
Publishing Group Inc
Reprinted 2011, 2012
Reprinted by Bloomsbury Academic 2013, 2014 (twice), 2015, 2016 (twice),
2017 (twice), 2018, 2019 (twice), 2020

Bloomsbury Publishing Inc does not have any control over, or responsibility for, any
third-party websites referred to or in this book. All internet addresses given in this
book were correct at the time of going to press. The author and publisher regret any
inconvenience caused if addresses have changed or sites have ceased to exist, but can accept
no responsibility for any such changes.

Wilcken, Hugo.
Low/Hugo Wilcken.
p.cm. – (33 1/3)
Includes bibliographical references (p.).
ISBN 0-8264-1684-5 (pbk.: alk. paper)
1. Bowie, David. 2. Bowie, David. Low. I. Title. II. Series.
ML420.B754W55 2005
782.42166'092–dc22

ISBN: PB: 978-0-8264-1684-1
ePDF: 978-1-4411-9955-3
ePUB: 978-1-4411-3129-4

Series: 33 1/3, volume 26

Printed and bound in the United States of America

To find out more about our authors and books visit www.bloomsbury.com
and sign up for our newsletters.

CONTENTS

acknowledgements

Thanks to my family, particularly Patrick Wilcken, for his help with research and critical reading of the text. Thanks also to David Barker, for commissioning the book; to Nick Currie, for an interesting exchange of e-mails; to Chris from menofmusic.com, for locating and sending me material; and to everyone else who helped in the writing of the work. And a special thank you to Julie Street, for her significant editorial input and all-round support.

This book is dedicated to the memory of my friend Peter Meyer (1964–2003).

introduction

I first heard *Low* in late 1979, soon after my fifteenth birthday. One of my older brothers had sent me a cassette, home-taped from the vinyl. I was far from my family and my native Australia doing a term of school in Dunkirk in northern France, ostensibly to learn French. Dunkirk was a grey simulacrum of a city. It had been destroyed during the Second World War, and entirely rebuilt afterwards according to the original plans. Every building contained the ghost of its bombed-out twin. At the city's edge, a wide desolate beach stretched out for miles. At low tide, you could see the wrecks of boats that had never made it across the Channel, during the desperate evacuation of Allied troops in 1940. Flanders is only twelve kilometres to the east, and the landscape around Dunkirk is similar—fluorescent green fields that are unrelentingly flat, quite disorientating for someone from hilly Sydney. In winter, the northern, pewter skies hung oppressively low, and the drizzle was constant. My French was approximate and communication difficult, accentuating the sense of isolation that is the natural state for a fifteen-year-old boy. Of course, *Low* was the perfect soundtrack.

Fifteen is the age of bedroom retreat, and three of the five *Low* songs with lyrics use withdrawal to a bedroom as a symbol for isolation. It's also the age of ravenous intellectual curiosity, of devouring books and art and music to access new worlds of the imagination. *Low* seemed to be a glimpse into such a world, one that I didn't really understand, subverting my expectations of what I'd understood a pop record should be. "Always Crashing in the Same Car" had the spooked feeling of a recurring dream; "A New Career in a New Town" had a yearning about it that looked both forward and back. The instrumentals on the second side weren't pop music at all, and had allusive titles such as the punning "Art Decade," "Weeping Wall" or "Subterraneans," which suggested fading civilisations gone to ground. The album left a haunting impression.

In the eighties, David Bowie forfeited a fair chunk of his artistic mystique in exchange for megastardom as a stadium entertainer, and my interest moved on to other things. Lately, he's redeemed himself somewhat, but it's only in the past few years that my attention turned back to what now seems to me to be a fascinating moment in the mid-seventies, when people like Bowie, Brian Eno or Kraftwerk were redefining what it meant to engage with the pop and rock genres. It was partly about injecting an experimental, European sensibility into a medium that was largely American in its conception. Of course, high and low art had been collapsing into each other ever since Warhol, Lichtenstein and the other pop art innovators had emerged in the early sixties. But if in the sixties it was art that was slumming it with pop aesthetics, the reverse was happening in the mid-seventies. Pop went arty. And *Low* marks the highpoint of this development, with its atmosphere of modernist alienation, its expressionism, its eclectic blend of R&B rhythms, electronics, minimalism and process-driven techniques, its suspicion of narrative.

I don't want to put *Low* into any sort of canon of great works. That seems to me to be imposing notions of worth from another age and a different cultural enterprise. Not a lot of modern culture can be treated in that way any more, and pop culture certainly can't. No single album can bear the weight of greatness, torn away from the support of all the other songs and all the other albums, the whole fabric of the hybrid culture that produced it. That's pop culture's strength, not its weakness. And that's why in this book I'm going to talk around *Low* almost as much as I talk about it—looking at how it relates to the other points on the cultural matrix, where it came from, how it fits with Bowie's artistic development. In short, what ingredients went into making an LP that Bowie once said captured "a sense of yearning for a future that we all knew would never come to pass."

from kether to melkuth

As far as the music goes, *Low* and its siblings were a direct follow-on from the title track of *Station to Station*. It's often struck me that there will usually be one track on any given album of mine which will be a fair indicator of the intent of the following album.

—David Bowie, 2001

I see *Low* as very much a continuation from *Station to Station*, which I think is one of the great records of all time.

—Brian Eno, 1999

The journey towards *Low* begins with the rattling pistons of a locomotive, opening the title track of David Bowie's previous album *Station to Station*, recorded in Los Angeles in late 1975. Retro steam train noises fade in then move across the aural landscape, literally, from the left channel to the right. (The album was actually recorded in quadra-phonic sound—one of those forgotten hi-fi innovations of the seventies—with the train circling its way around all four speakers.) Bowie had pinched the train noises from a radio sound effects record, and had then further treated them in the studio, using equalisation and unconventional phasing methods, giving them that skewed, not-quite-real feeling that is emblematic of this strange album.

Those train sounds herald the theme of restless travel as a spiritual metaphor, also present on *Low* and the following albums of what Bowie calls his "Berlin triptych" (*Low*, *"Heroes"*, *Lodger*). Sonically, *Station to Station* is a voyage in itself, journeying from the mid-seventies funk of the New York disco scene to the pulsing *motorik* beat of experimental German bands such as Neu!, Can or Kraftwerk. In fact, those opening sound effects are pretty much an *hommage* to Kraftwerk's unlikely 1974 hit *Autobahn*, which begins with a car revving up and driving off, the sound also crossing over from left to right channel.

Like *Autobahn*, *Station to Station* is a veritable epic in rock/pop terms. Clocking in at over ten minutes, this is the longest track Bowie has ever written (the instrumental intro-duction alone outdistances most songs on *Low*). It's over a minute before Earl Slick's guitar kicks in, mimicking at first a train whistle, then the clunking sounds of engines and wheels on track. "I got some quite extraordinary things out of Earl Slick," Bowie has said. "I think it captured his imagination to make noises on guitar, and textures, rather than playing the right notes." That experimental groping towards sound as texture rather than chords and melody is definitely there all right, even if it's not really followed through on the rest of the album.

From there on, there's a gradual building up of instrumentation. A metronomic two-note piano figure sets up a self-consciously mechanical beat, which is almost immediately opposed by the R&B rhythm section of Dennis Davis (drums), George Murray (bass) and Carlos Alomar (guitar). Alomar's funk licks battle it out with Slick's noise guitar, while the mellotron overlays a melody line against a chaos of bizarre industrial sound effects.

Already, before Bowie has sung a note, a musical agenda is being laid down. Alomar sees it as "funky on the bass, but everything on top was just rock 'n' roll." That captures part of what it was: funk instrumentation with European-style lead melody. For Bowie, "*Station to Station* was really the rock-format version of what was to come on *Low* and *"Heroes"*. I was at the time well into German electronic music—Can, and all that. And Kraftwerk had made a big impression on me." What Bowie was working his way towards was some kind of hybridisation between the R&B he'd already pastiched on *Young Americans* and the textures and beats of the German *Kosmische* bands (of whom more later), along with other experimentalists in both the rock and classical worlds. That hybridisation is mostly left suggested on *Station to Station*. But new territory is clearly being marked out, quite different from earlier successes like *Hunky Dory* or *Ziggy Stardust,* which, from a musical perspective, remain conventional slices of English rock.

After the extended funk/industrial workout, Bowie's vocals crash in, and things start to get weird. The first half-dozen lines pack in a bewildering array of allusions to gnosticism, black magic and the kabbala (a medieval school of Jewish mysticism). "The return of the thin white duke, throwing darts in lovers' eyes / The return of the thin white duke, making sure white stains." This is for initiates only—the sexual/drug connotations of the "white stains" may be obvious enough, but the casual listener will hardly pick up that it's also the title of an obscure book of poetry by the notorious English occultist Aleister Crowley (1875–1947). "Throwing darts in lovers' eyes" also references Crowley, alluding to a no doubt apocryphal incident in 1918, when Crowley killed a young couple in a magical rite that involved hurling darts.

A mangled version of a famous line from Shakespeare's *Tempest* ("such is the stuff from where dreams are woven") recalls another magician, Prospero, who is of course a duke, banished to an island ("tall in my room overlooking the ocean," as Bowie puts it). And the "magical movement from kether to melkuth" suggests more than a passing interest in *The Tree of Life*, a kabbalistic treatise written by Crowley disciple Israel Regardie. The Tree of Life is a mystical diagram in which *kether* represents the godhead and *melkuth* the physical world, while the magical movement between the two enacts the Gnostic myth of the Fall. In the booklet of the current remaster of the album, an anaemic Bowie is to be seen sketching out the Tree of Life on a studio floor.

It doesn't end there: there are plenty of other occult allusions to be teased out—"lost in my circle," "flashing no colour," "sunbirds to soar with" all have their specific mystical meanings. According to Bowie, the song is almost a "step-by-step interpretation of the kabbala, although absolutely no one else realised that at the time, of course." That's something of an exaggeration—intellectually, the mix of references is rather confused, although it works extremely well on a poetic level.

Crowleyism was not a rock novelty in 1975. Led Zeppelin's Jimmy Page was a disciple; Can's extraordinary *Tago Mago* (1971) alludes to Crowley; and arguably the most famous LP ever, *Sgt Pepper*, depicts Crowley on its cover. Previous Bowie songs also reference occultism ("Quicksand" namechecks Crowley, Himmler and the Golden Dawn society of which both were members), and traces of it subsist on later albums, including *Low*. But never was it so blatant as on *Station to Station*. What are we to make of this? Certain critics make a great deal indeed. The late Ian McDonald (whose *Revolution in the Head* remains the benchmark of Beatles literature) grandly depicts Bowie as a Prospero figure executing an "exorcism of the self, of mind, of the past….Bowie has ascended the Tree of Life; now he wants to come down to earth, to love," and to "cast his occult *grimoire* into the ocean."

There's another, rather more prosaic reading of these black magic ramblings. "It's not the side-effects of the cocaine," Bowie opines a little further on in the song, but I think we can safely assume a case of protesting too much. Because the *Station to Station* sessions represent the high-water mark of Bowie's prodigious drug intake. By this stage, Bowie had practically stopped eating and was subsisting on a diet of milk, cocaine and four packets of Gitanes a day. He was leading a vampyric existence of blinds-drawn seclusion in his Hollywood mansion, spliced with all-night sessions in the studio. There were times when he'd start recording in the evening then work all the way through until ten in the morning—and when told that the studio had been booked for another band, he'd simply call up for studio time elsewhere on the spot and start work again immediately. Other times, he could vanish altogether: "We show up at the studio," says Slick. " 'Where is he?' He shows up maybe five or six hours late. Sometimes he wouldn't show up at all." At this stage, Bowie could go five or six days without sleep, the point at which reality and imagination become irretrievably blurred: "By the end of the week my whole life would be transformed into this bizarre nihilistic fantasy world of oncoming doom, mythological characters and imminent totalitarianism."

Essentially, Bowie was suffering from severe bouts of cocaine psychosis, a condition very similar to schizophrenia, with its highly distorted perceptions of reality, hallucinations, affectlessness and a marked tendency towards magical thinking. His interviews of the time are classics of messianic delusion, as he raves on about Hitler being the first rock star, or his own political ambitions ("I'd love to enter politics. I will one day. I'd adore to be Prime Minister. And yes, I believe very strongly in fascism."). The flipside of messianic fantasy is of course paranoid delusion, which Bowie also displayed in spades. He imagined one of his advisers was a CIA agent; a backing singer was apparently a vampire. During one interview, Bowie suddenly leapt up and pulled down the blind: "I've got to do this," he jabbered. "I just saw a body fall." He proceeded to light a black candle then blow it out. "It's only a protection. I've been getting a little trouble from the neighbours." How much of all this was theatre and how much delusion? Bowie was evidently past making such distinctions. His wife of the time, Angie, recounts getting a phone call from him one day in 1975; Bowie was somewhere in Los Angeles with a warlock and two witches who wanted to steal his semen for a black magic ritual. "He was talking in slurred, hushed tones, and hardly making any sense and he was crazed with fear."

Bowie was quite capable of camping up his "weirdness" when it suited him. And yet if only a quarter of the stories circulating about him from this time are true—of his keeping his urine in the fridge, of black magic altars in the living room, of professional exorcisms of his swimming pool and so on—this would still be a man with serious mental health issues, to say the least. On top of his cocaine addiction and related delusions, Bowie was also physically cut off from any kind of "normal" existence. Life at Doheny Drive, where he'd taken up residence, resembled a kind of court, peopled with musicians, dealers, lovers, and a whole host of parasitic shysters and hangers-on. His assistant Corinne "Coco" Schwab acted as a gatekeeper, sorting out the logistics of his life, insulating him from situations and people that upset him. His ability to do anything for himself had become severely restrained. Fame, cocaine, isolation and Los Angeles ("the least suitable place on earth for a person to go in search of identity and stability," as he'd put it later) had all conspired to spin Bowie off into a very dark place indeed.

Given this state of affairs, the wonder is that Bowie got anything done in the studio at all. And, in fact, by *Station to Station* there's very much a sense of the artist as well as the man in crisis. It had been a year since the *Young Americans* sessions, and he'd done very little recording since then. In May 1975 he'd taken his friend Iggy Pop in to record some material, but the session had quickly become chaotic, with Pop and Bowie even coming to blows at one stage. This was at the height of his "stick insect paranoia look," according to guitarist James Williamson, who'd found Bowie slumped at the control booth, enveloped in a hideous wall of distorted noise.

For *Station to Station*, Bowie went into the studio with only two songs, both of which were eventually changed beyond recognition. He was accustomed to working extremely quickly—the bulk of *Ziggy Stardust*, for instance, was done in a two-week period, itself coming only weeks after the recording of *Hunky Dory*. By contrast, the *Station to Station* sessions stretched out over two and a half months, yielding just five original compositions and a histrionic cover version of "Wild Is the Wind."

"You retain a superficial hold on reality so that you can get through the things that you know are absolutely necessary for your survival," Bowie mused in 1993. "But when that starts to break up, which inevitably it does—around late 1975 everything was starting to break up—I would work at songs for hours and hours and days and days and then realise after a few days that I had done absolutely nothing. I thought I'd been working and working, but I'd only been rewriting the first four bars or something. And I hadn't got anywhere. I couldn't believe it! I'd been working on it for a week! I hadn't got past four bars! And I'd realise that I'd been changing those four bars around, doing them backwards, splitting them up and doing the end first. An obsession with detail had taken over." It was yet another consequence of the psychosis, and that eerie, overwrought quality is all over *Station to Station*. It's the cocaine album *par excellence*, in its slow, hypnotic rhythms, its deranged romantic themes, its glacial alienation, its dialogue with God ("Word on a Wing"), in the pure white lines of the album cover, in the hi-fi sheen that's clean enough to snort off.

But to get back to the title track. As the occult incantations of the first section end, the distorted train sounds make a brief return, and then comes a bridge at 5:17. The song abruptly switches tempo to a Neu!-like *motorik* chug; the instrumentation simplifies; and new melody lines break in, almost as if it were another song entirely—as it probably was originally (not a lot of detail is known about these sessions, due to the cocaine habits and memory holes of just about everyone involved). Now we're looking back to some kind of lost idyll, a time when "there were mountains and mountains and sunbirds to soar with, and once I could never be down." It's here that the restless, questing theme makes its appearance—"got to keep searching and searching and what will I be believing and who will connect me with love?"

A final section kicks in at 6:03, the rhythm changing yet again to disco-inflected beats, with rock guitar and piano hurtling along on top. "It's not the side-effects of the cocaine," Bowie now delusionally meditates. "I'm thinking that it must be love." It's as if the narrator is so alienated that he's come out the other side, into something approaching passion (the title, Bowie has said, refers to the Stations of the Cross). And now a new incantation repeats itself to fade: "It's too late to be grateful, it's too late to be late again / It's too late to be hateful, the European canon is here." "It was like a plea to come back to Europe," Bowie commented a few years later. "It was one of those self-chat things one has with oneself from time to time."

That last lyric points to what the track achieved sonically. The train has travelled from occult-tinged, post-Manson Los Angeles towards a certain modernist Europe and its avant-garde pretensions, its experimental song structures, its fascination with sound as texture. A Europe where traditional popular music (British music hall, French *chanson*, German cabaret) had always privileged exaggeration and role-playing over authenticity and self-expression. "Towards the end of my stay in America," Bowie has said, "I realised that what I had to do was to experiment. To discover new forms of writing. To evolve, in fact, a new musical language. That's what I set out to do. That's why I returned to Europe." The Rimbaud-esque desire to create a new language is perhaps the upside of the messianism. There's an irony in his inversion of the order of things: the conventional spiritual journey is from the Old World to the New, striking out for fresh horizons and frontiers. It's the troubled aesthetes—Henry James, T. S. Eliot, Ezra Pound—who make the reverse trip.

This struggle towards Europe (along with the schizophrenic flavour of the two albums) is what connects *Station to Station* to its successor *Low*. The link is further underlined by the album cover, a still from Bowie's first (and by a long chalk his best) movie, *The Man Who Fell to Earth*, which Bowie worked on directly prior to the *Station to Station* sessions. It shows him as the alien Thomas Jerome Newton entering his spaceship (in reality an anechoic chamber). The current reissue of the album has a full-length colour image, but on the original release it was cropped and black and white, giving it an austere, expressionist flavour redolent of the European modernism of the 1920s and the photography of Man Ray. The stark, red sans sérif typography—the album title and artist are run together (**STATIONTOSTATION-DAVIDBOWIE**)—adds to the retro-modernist feel. Bowie himself hovers somewhere between America and Europe, his hair in a James Dean quiff, his tieless white shirt severely buttoned to the neck. The cover of *Low*, too, is a treated still from *The Man Who Fell to Earth*.

the visitor

In December 1975, shortly after he'd signed off on *Station to Station*, Bowie was back at work on a soundtrack for *The Man Who Fell to Earth*—although ultimately it wasn't used in the film, and remains to this day unreleased. If *Station to Station* laid down the artistic groundwork for *Low*, its actual genesis came in these soundtrack sessions. Various *Low* tracks are reported to have been recycled from this time— Brian Eno has said that "Weeping Wall" started life there, although Bowie himself claims that "the only hold-over from the proposed soundtrack that I actually used was the reverse bass part in 'Subterraneans.'" He is perhaps not the most reliable witness to the lost weekend of 1975 (Bowie on *Station to Station:* "I know it was recorded in LA because I read it was"), but other hold-over candidates do seem to me to be ruled out on internal evidence.

Bowie worked with Paul Buckmaster (producer of his

1969 "Space Oddity" hit), who brought in a cello to accompany Bowie's guitar, synthesisers and drum machines. The sessions (at Bowie's Bel Air home) produced five or six working tracks, recorded on a TEAC four-track tape recorder. According to Buckmaster, the two were very taken at the time with Kraftwerk's recently released *Radio-Activity*. This album caught Kraftwerk at a transitional phase of their career, channelling free-form experimentalism towards more tightly controlled, robotic rhythms that are like the sonic equivalent of a Mondrian painting. *Radio-Activity* is a clear influence on *Low*, with its mix of pop hooks, unsettling sound effects, retro-modernism; its introspection and emotional flatness. The theremin-sounding synths of "Always Crashing in the Same Car" and the electronic interludes on "A New Career in a New Town" in particular have a *Radio-Activity* feel to them.

Apart from that early run-through of "Subterraneans," then, these sessions' real contribution to *Low* was that they got Bowie thinking about (and creating) atmospheric, "mood" music for the first time. In a career of over a decade, Bowie had yet to record a single instrumental piece. In this respect, the loghorrea of *Station to Station*—with its lumber room of loosely connected images—looks backwards rather than forwards, since more than half the tracks on *Low* ended up lyric-less, and the others are pretty monosyllabic. Until *Low*, Bowie had tended to follow some sort of narrative line, however elusive. On *Low*, even on the songs with lyrics, that narrative impulse largely falls away. And it was during the *Man Who Fell to Earth* sessions that, he later said, he first got the idea of hooking up with Brian Eno at some point.

There are conflicting accounts as to why the soundtrack project was abandoned. According to Bowie, his manager, Michael Lippman, had promised to secure him the rights to score the film and he'd started recording on that basis. When later told that his work would be competing in a three-way pitch, he withdrew from the process in a fury. That account doesn't quite square with those of others involved. According to Harry Maslin, who co-produced *Station to Station*, Bowie was by this stage so burned out that he couldn't focus on the work properly. Buckmaster seems to agree, recalling one session where Bowie had practically overdosed and had to be helped out of the studio. "I considered the music to be demo-ish and not final, although we were supposed to be making it final," Buckmaster told Bowie biographer David Buckley. "All we produced was something that was substandard, and [the film's director] Nic Roeg turned it down on those grounds."

John Phillips, who ended up doing the soundtrack, tells yet a different story: "Roeg wanted banjos and folk music and Americana for the film, which was about an alien who drops from the sky into the southwest. 'David really can't do that kind of thing,' Roeg said." This seems to me a better explanation for the rejection of the Bowie soundtrack—*The*

Man Who Fell to Earth has a sci-fi premise but isn't really a sci-fi film and a spacey, futuristic soundtrack would have set the wrong tone. As for the quality of Bowie's work, those who did hear it were impressed. Phillips found it "haunting and beautiful, with chimes, Japanese bells, and what sounded like electronic wind and waves." Bowie had the soundtrack with him during the *Low* sessions for work on "Subterraneans," and at one stage played it to the musicians: "It was excellent," recalled guitarist Ricky Gardiner, "quite unlike anything else he's done." Months later, Bowie sent Roeg a copy of *Low*, with a note that said: "This is what I wanted to do for the soundtrack."

The Man Who Fell to Earth was English filmmaker Nic Roeg's fourth movie. In the prime of his career in the mid-seventies, he'd received widespread acclaim for arthouse classics such as *Walkabout* and *Don't Look Now*. And he'd already initiated one rock star (Mick Jagger) into the world of acting, on his directorial debut *Performance*. But for Bowie, *The Man Who Fell to Earth* turned out to be more than just his first major acting job. In many respects, Thomas Jerome Newton, the part he plays, was Nic Roeg's projection of Bowie, and Bowie, in turn, confessed to "being Newton for six months" after the movie shoot, wearing Newton's clothes and striking his poses. ("I'd been offered a couple of scripts but I chose this one because it was the only one where I didn't have to sing or look like David Bowie," he said at the time. "Now I think that David Bowie looks like

Newton.") Roeg had first wanted Peter O'Toole for the role but became interested in Bowie after seeing a documentary that Alan Yentob had made for the BBC arts programme *Omnibus*. It was entitled *Cracked Actor*, and caught a pale, stick-thin Bowie as he toured America. It impressed Roeg greatly, to the extent that a scene in which Bowie is having some sort of psychotic episode in the back of a limo in New York was re-created for the movie, with the same chauffeur and even snatches of the dialogue reprised. Other self-referential moments make clear the link between Bowie and the role he's playing. Like Bowie, Newton creates music, and near the end of the film, he makes an album of spectral sounds entitled *The Visitor*. The scene in which a character buys this album shows a record store display promoting Bowie's *Young Americans* in the background. An early screenplay apparently used Bowie lyrics as well.

The movie is about an alien who travels to Earth from a drought-stricken planet, where he has left a wife and child. Using his superior knowledge, he starts up a high-tech corporation to earn the money he needs to build a spaceship, which would ship water to save his planet. Into his reclusive life comes Mary-Lou, an elevator operator, who introduces Newton to TV and alcohol. Meanwhile, his phenomenal rise to power sparks interest from government agents, who find out about his space project and determine to stop it. They imprison Newton in a penthouse and subject him to medical examinations. Eventually they lose interest in him; Mary-

Lou tracks him down and he escapes. He records *The Visitor*, which he hopes his wife, who may already be dead, will hear. Knowing he can neither go back home nor save his dying family, Newton descends into self-pity and alcohol. In a sense, he has become human.

Bowie is not called upon to act in any conventional sense (and when he occasionally has to, the results are fairly lame). He merely projects an otherworldliness that's already there in the alienation that's the result of rock star fame, drug abuse and a romantic conception of the creative life. "The basic premise is of a man forced to be in a position where he has to enter a society, not letting too much be known because then he'd be in continual isolation," explains Nic Roeg. "It had to be a secret self, a secret person. Emotionally, I think a lot of these thoughts appealed to David." Newton is like a refugee, "an astronaut of inner space rather than outer space. I remember David and I talking about that theme."

The second, "ambient" side of *Low* is partly about exploring Newton's vast interior landscapes, as Bowie's note to Roeg implies. The fact that two of Bowie's albums and numerous singles bear images from the film illustrate its importance. The role was a perfect feint for the Bowie persona, crystallising the metaphor of the alien, which Bowie continued to both nurture and fight against (his uninspiring "regular guy" schtick of the 1980s was something of a reaction to it). As late as 1997, the chosen title of his album

Earthling resonates with an irony that goes back to *The Man Who Fell to Earth*.

one magical movement

Station to Station was released in late January 1976. If it didn't do quite as well as its predecessor, *Young Americans*, it was still very much a commercial as well as a critical success, spending several weeks at the top of the charts and yielding a top ten single on both sides of the Atlantic ("Golden Years").

Following its release, Bowie decided (or was persuaded) to tour the album across the States, and then Europe. His previous foray into the concert halls had resulted in something of an overblown prog rock absurdity, with an elaborate, hugely expensive set. For the new tour, Bowie wanted something far simpler, if no less theatrical. The only real prop would be vast banks of harsh white light, creating a sort of Brechtian distance, and continuing the artistic journey back to Europe: "I wanted to go back to a kind of Expressionist German film look," Bowie has said. "A feeling of a Berlinesque performer—black waistcoat, black trousers, white shirt, and the lighting of, say, Fritz Lang, or Pabst. A black-and-white-movies look, but with an intensity that was sort of aggressive. I think for me, personally, theatrically, that was the most successful tour I've ever done." In the dramatic play of white light and shadow, others saw more than a hint of Nuremberg as well—an impression not discouraged by Bowie's provocative pronunciations on fascism during this period.

All in all, it was a distinctly arty affair. The show opened with a projection of Luis Buñuel's 1920s surrealist classic, *Le Chien Andalou*—the one with the excruciating eyeball-slicing sequence—which was accompanied by tracks from Kraftwerk's equally arty, equally un-rock *Radio-Activity* album. (Bowie had invited Kraftwerk to open for him, but they'd declined the offer, or perhaps hadn't even responded to it.) Bowie himself performed dressed in the style of a dissolute pre-war aristocrat. He was playing the role of the thin white duke referenced on *Station to Station*'s title track—"a very nasty character indeed," Bowie admitted later. The thin white duke was less sketched-out than other characters Bowie had inhabited; he was a chilly, Aryan elitist with Nietzchean overtones, and the morbid self-absorption of a nineteenth-century German romantic.

It was a formidable piece of expressionist theatre that received adulatory reviews. And yet, in the midst of this artistic success, and despite the iron self-discipline needed to formulate it and carry it off, Bowie actually seemed to be as deranged as ever. In Stockholm he regaled a journalist with the script he was writing about Goebbels, and the land he was going to buy to start up his own country. The messianic delusions had hardly abated; quite the contrary: "As I see it I am the only alternative for the premier in England. I believe Britain could benefit from a fascist leader. After all, fascism is really nationalism." Bowie later passed this off as provocation, which it obviously was, although the line between delusion and provocation had by then become gossamer-thin.

"That whole *Station to Station* tour was done under duress," Bowie later said. "I was out of my mind totally, completely crazed. Really. But the main thing I was functioning on, as far as that whole thing about Hitler and Rightism was concerned, was mythology." Essentially, Bowie's interest in fascism wasn't really political, it was just another offshoot of his loopy obsession with the occult: "The search for the Holy Grail. That was my real fascination with the Nazis. The whole thing that in the thirties they had come over to Glastonbury Tor. And naïvely, politically, I didn't even think about what they had done….It's hard to see that you could get involved with all that and not see the implications of what you were getting into. But at the time I was obsessed with the idea that the Nazis were looking for the Holy Grail."

On February 11, after his Los Angeles concert, Bowie

met up with the novelist Christopher Isherwood, a writer he admired. Isherwood's best known novels, *Mr Norris Changes Trains* and *Goodbye to Berlin*, are in essence autobiographies of a bohemian young Englishman in Weimar-era Berlin (the latter was made into the movie *Cabaret*, starring Liza Minelli and Michael York). The Berlin cabaret life described by Isherwood—dancing in the face of imminent catastrophe—appealed to Bowie in the same way that Evelyn Waugh's *Vile Bodies* had appealed and had prompted him to write "Aladdin Sane." And of course it was exactly that kind of atmosphere that had influenced the look of the *Station to Station* tour. The two talked at length, with Bowie pumping Isherwood for stories about Berlin—clearly already on his mind as a possible European refuge. Isherwood was rather discouraging: Berlin was quite boring even then, he told Bowie. And the decadent bohemia he portrayed in his books? "Young Bowie," Isherwood waspishly pronounced, "people forget that I'm a very good fiction writer." Nevertheless, Bowie would end up living fifteen minutes' walk from Isherwood's old Berlin flat. And to some extent he'd play the same sort of "decadent Englishman abroad" games as the young Isherwood had in the early thirties (with Iggy Pop as Sally Bowles to Bowie's "Herr Issyvoo").

There were more Nazi shenanigans on April 2, when returning from a trip to Moscow, Bowie was strip-searched at the Russian/Polish border, and had biographies of Speer and Goebbels confiscated by customs officials (Bowie claimed it was research material for the Goebbels film). The *Station to Station* tour rolled into Berlin a week later, on April 10. Bowie had been there once before, to perform on West German TV in 1969, but didn't know the city. He went into sightseeing mode, taking his presidential open-roof Mercedes on a tour of East Berlin, and then to Hitler's bunker. Long after he moved to Berlin and had presumably outgrown his occult fixations, Bowie remained fascinated by the city's Nazi past, seeking out remaining examples of Speer's architecture, visiting the former Gestapo headquarters and so on. The Berlin tour stop found Bowie already slipping into the Isherwood role: it was then that he met transsexual cabaret performer Romy Haag (described by one biographer as "like Sally Bowles, only more so"), with whom he would later have a well-publicised affair.

Back in England for the first time in over two years, Bowie courted yet more controversy at London's Victoria Station by seemingly giving a Hitler salute (May 2). Bowie claims that the photographer caught him mid-wave, which is probably true, but he'd certainly opened himself up to the misrepresentation. An interview with Jean Rook in the *Daily Express* catches him furiously back-pedalling on his fascist pronouncements of a few days before. Here, the emaciated, Dracula-pale Bowie comes across as worrying and charming in equal parts, talking of himself in the third person, painting the portrait of a Pierrot "putting over the great sadness of 1976." He describes his Ziggy Stardust look as "a cross between Nijinsky and Woolworth's"—a beautifully pithy summary of what so much of Bowie had been about.

talking through the gloom

Bowie gave a series of triumphant, sell-out concerts at Wembley (May 3–8), to widespread critical acclaim. Brian Eno attended one of them (May 7), and the two met up backstage after the show. They'd run into each other a couple of times before, but weren't yet friends. Eno's old band Roxy Music had once opened for Bowie, back in 1973. In the early seventies Bowie and Roxy Music had had much in common, in their English art-school pretensions, their foregrounding of style and pastiche, their swimming against the tide of "authentic" singer-songwriters. Since leaving Roxy, Eno had released a number of solo albums that moved from English rock to the outer reaches of pop experimentalism and hybridisation. He'd set up the Obscure record label, which further collapsed high and low art distinctions, releasing milestone contemporary classical works such as Gavin Bryars's *Jesus' Blood Never Failed*

Me Yet. Independently from Bowie, he'd also picked up on the German experimental scene. Bowie has occasionally claimed to have introduced Eno to the so-called "krautrock" bands, but the fact is that by then Eno had already worked with electronic pioneers Harmonia, both on stage and in the studio. In fact, one of the stories of the whole mid-seventies art rock phenomenon is the way the various players converge on similar ideas and hybrid forms, making the question of who really influenced whom difficult to say the least, and probably meaningless.

After the concert, Bowie and Eno drove back together to where Bowie was staying in Maida Vale and talked into the night. Bowie told Eno he'd been listening to *Discreet Music* (1975). "He said he'd been playing it non-stop on his American tour," Eno recalled, "and naturally flattery always endears you to someone. I thought: God, he must be smart!" *Discreet Music* was Eno's latest release at the time, and is not a pop record at all. One side comprises different versions of Pachelbel's *Canon*, processed via various algorithmic transformations, to arrive at something sounding a little similar to Gavin Bryars's *The Sinking of the Titanic*. Bowie may have been impressed with it, but it's not the Eno album with which *Low* has the most in common. Eno again: "I know he liked *Another Green World* a lot, and he must have realised that there were these two parallel streams of working going on in what I was doing, and when you find someone with the same problems you tend to become friendly with them."

Another Green World (1975) has a different feel to *Low*, but it deploys some of the same strategies. It mixes songs that have recognisable pop structures with other, short, abstract pieces that Eno called "ambient"—with the emphasis not on melody or beat, but on atmosphere and texture. These intensely beautiful fragments fade in then out, as if they were merely the visible part of a vast submarine creation; they are like tiny glimpses into another world. On the more conventional tracks, different genres juxtapose, sometimes smoothly, sometimes not—jazzy sounds cohering with pop hooks but struggling against intrusive synthetic sound effects. The end result is a moodily enigmatic album of real power and ingenuity. One structural difference between the two albums, though, is that while Eno interspersed the "textural" pieces across *Another Green World*, Bowie separated them out and put them on another side, which provides *Low* with a sort of metanarrative.

Eno styled himself as a "non-musician"; he even tried (and failed) to have that put on his passport as his profession. Of course he had plenty of chops, but his insight was to consider the studio as the primary instrument of creativity (he'd already written an essay entitled "The Studio as a Compositional Tool"). This puts the focus on context rather than content, on the sonic surface rather than deep melodic structure. It ran up against a very different and perhaps more prevalent "rootsy" approach to rock, where musical virtuosity was privileged and studio "trickery" frowned upon; where the studio was viewed more like a camera taking a snapshot of a performance. Eno's interventionist vision owes something to the studio experimentation of mid-sixties pop but also to the avant-garde process-driven techniques of people like Karlheinz Stockhausen or John Cage, pioneers of the use of tape collages and loops, prepared instruments, electronics and randomness, in the 1950s and 1960s. But the excitement of music in the early seventies lay not so much with the dryly cerebral work of Stockhausen (who has always been more admired than listened to) but with more popular forms which could be invigorated with the experimentalism of the academic traditions. Bowie had long been interested in Eno's approach to the studio, and had occasionally used similar techniques—the Burroughsian cut-up experiments on *Diamond Dogs* were heading in the same direction, deliberately using disorientation as a means of hitting upon something new and different.

Bowie and Eno agreed to keep in touch. Meanwhile, the *Station to Station* tour shunted on to its terminus: Paris. Bowie travelled there by train, under the name Stenton Jones (Stenton being the middle name of his dead father), and gave two concerts at the Pavillon de Paris (May 15–18). He threw a glamorous end-of-tour party at the Alcazar nightclub, attended by the great and good of the entertainment-industrial complex, plus an array of fashionable creatures from the Euro demi-monde (including Romy Haag, with whom Bowie ended the night). At another Bowie-organised party in Paris, this time at the Ange Bleu, Kraftwerk had put in an appearance, receiving a five-minute standing ovation as they entered blank-faced and got up in full-blown 1930s retro style, like the musical equivalents of Gilbert and George. Bowie was enthralled: "Look how they are, they are fantastic!" he kept repeating to Iggy Pop, who had accompanied Bowie on the tour.

Bowie had already met Kraftwerk frontmen Florian Schneider and Ralf Hütter in Los Angeles. According to Schneider and Hütter, they'd talked about working together; according to Bowie, they hadn't. Whatever the case, nothing ever came of it, but Bowie saw them socially a few times once he'd moved to Germany. These days, Bowie is a touch equivocal about Kraftwerk's musical influence on him, although there are some undeniably Kraftwerkian moments on *Low*. But it's true that Bowie's and Kraftwerk's conceptions of rhythm diverge wildly. *Low* is a meeting of the synthetic and the organic—Bowie was welding R&B beats to electronic soundscapes. But Kraftwerk were in the process of eliminating the human altogether from the beat (their robot rhythms ultimately bled back into black music through house and techno, but that's another story).

The significance of Kraftwerk at this stage of Bowie's career was more general. It was the 1974 release of *Autobahn* that had turned his attention back to Europe, and to electronic music: "What I was passionate about in relation to

Kraftwerk was their singular determination to stand apart from stereotypical American chord sequences and their wholehearted embrace of a European sensibility displayed through their music," Bowie said in 2001. "This was their very important influence on me."

Kraftwerk and the *Kosmische* bands of the early seventies belonged to a generation of Germans that "had no fathers, only grandfathers," as film director Werner Herzog once put it. "Because of the war," Kraftwerk frontman Ralf Hütter told a French journalist in 1978, "and the rupture it caused with the past, we no longer had a tradition to respect, we were free to experiment. And we weren't taken in by the myth of the pop star either. We'd seen enough of that in the 1930s." That rupture propelled German artists forwards into the future, but sometimes also backwards, skipping a generation to before the Nazi catastrophe, to the false dawn of the Weimar years or the German Romanticism of the previous century. Kraftwerk actually went both ways, using electronics and avant-garde techniques to create a "European industrial folk music" that conjures up a largely pre-war world of futuristic optimism. Band member Wolfgang Flür explains, "All of us in the group are children who were born straight after World War II. So, we had no musical or pop culture of our own, there was nothing behind us, there was the war, and before the war we had only the German folk music. In the 1920s or 1930s melodies were developed and these became culture that we worked from. So, I think it was in us, ever since we were born; I cannot explain us, but it is us. It is romantic, childish, maybe, it is naïve, but I cannot do anything about it. It's in me."

Kraftwerk's albums evoke a time when *autobahns* were a novelty; when travelling across Europe in a steam train was the epitome of glamour. They look back to the golden age of the radio, or the futurist visions of a 1920s movie like *Metropolis*. (More recently, there's been their twenty-year obsession with cycling, reducing the industrial fantasy of mechanical salvation to its simplest expression.) This nostalgia for a future that never happened was something that Bowie also picked up on; it's a sadness that informs the second sides of *Low* and its successor *"Heroes"*. At heart, it's very much a form of Romanticism (Kraftwerk signal this with the title of their 1977 track "Franz Schubert").

For a couple of years, Bowie's and Kraftwerk's careers seemed to intertwine. While Bowie was at work on *Low*, Kraftwerk were in the studio recording their groundbreaking *Trans-Europe Express*. An ambiguously kitsch photo of the group looking like a 1930s string quartet adorns the album cover. The title track cheekily namechecks both Bowie and his own "train" album ("from station to station to Düsseldorf city, meet Iggy Pop and David Bowie"); Bowie returned the favour on *"Heroes"* ("V2-Schneider"). Both Bowie and Kraftwerk conceived of their act as a whole—the music, the clothes, the artwork, the concerts, the interviews, all integrated and self-referring. They both nodded to pan-Europeanism, recording versions of their songs in French, German and English. Both nurtured a camp sensibility, working the delicate seam that lies between irony and earnestness. Both blended postmodern pastiche with a retro-modernist aesthetic. Both made emotional music by seeming to negate emotion. Seen through the prism of psychiatry, the work of both comes across as rather autistic (Bowie's autism is schizophrenic; Kraftwerk's obsessive-compulsive).

what can i do about my dreams?

In mid May, Bowie and Iggy Pop retired to the picturesque Château d'Hérouville, forty kilometres northwest of Paris, to rest up for a few days after the tour. The Château had been converted into studios by the well-known French film composer Michel Magne in 1969. While winding down there with Iggy, Bowie met up with the Château's manager and chief sound engineer Laurent Thibault, former bassist with the ultimate prog rock group Magma. The two talked late into the night. Much to Thibault's surprise, Bowie seemed well acquainted with Magma's peculiar oeuvre, which mostly consists of a series of concept albums about a planet called Kobaia—with many of the songs sung in native Kobaian. By the end of the night, Bowie had agreed to put down two hundred thousand francs to book the studios for the months of July and September (they were already taken for August). He'd already recorded *Pin-Ups* there, in 1973, and would eventually record most of *Low* at the Château as well.

From there, Bowie moved to a large house at Clos-des-Mésanges, near Vevey, Switzerland. The move had been engineered by his wife, Angie, partly to get him away from Los Angeles, but largely for tax reasons. Bowie was supposedly settling down to family life with his five-year-old son and wife. But by this stage, their marriage (outrageously open even by seventies rock marriage standards) had more or less broken down in a morass of recriminations and jealousies. Angie had in particular taken against Bowie's assistant Corinne Schwab, whom Bowie used to shield himself against the people he didn't want to see. "Coco kept the irritating people out of his life," his friend and producer Tony Visconti said in 1986, "and Angie had become one of them." Often, Bowie would simply disappear altogether without telling Angie, sometimes to Berlin, and with only Coco in the know. It enraged Angie. The couple's living arrangements became increasingly complicated; while Angie was away in London, Bowie would stay at the house, but when she was home, he'd book into a nearby hotel.

The idea had been to relax after the tour, but Bowie was clearly the sort who thrived on nervous energy, not relaxation. At Clos-des-Mésanges he amassed a library of 5,000 books and threw himself into reading them. Bowie had always been the intellectually curious autodidact, having left school at sixteen. But now it became something of an obsession. During the tour, Bowie had travelled around Europe in a kind of cultural rage, going to concerts, visiting galleries, learning everything he could about art, classical music and literature. It was a reaction against America, but there was also an element of replacing one mania for another (albeit far healthier) one.

A life of leisure in the Swiss Alps for the workaholic Bowie was another mirage, and when Iggy Pop showed up they began to rehearse what would result in Iggy's first solo venture, *The Idiot*, produced and cowritten by Bowie. He had admired Iggy's proto-punk band the Stooges from early on; had got them signed to his then manager's company, Mainman; had mixed the classic Stooges album *Raw Power;* had continually boosted Iggy Pop in the press. The two had become close in Los Angeles, when a washed-up Iggy Pop had checked himself into a mental asylum. "I think he respected me for putting myself in a loony bin," Iggy said in 1977. "He was the only guy who came to visit me. Nobody else came…nobody. Not even my so-called friends in LA… but David came." (At this time, back in England, Bowie's schizophrenic half-brother, Terry, had already been interned in a mental institution for some years.)

Various studio sessions during 1975 had produced little of worth (there'd been the dirge-like "Moving On," never released, plus a couple of tracks that ended up on *Lust For Life*, changed beyond recognition). But Bowie had invited Iggy on the *Station to Station* tour, and early on in the soundchecks they'd come up with "Sister Midnight," based around a Carlos Alomar riff. Bowie had written the first verse and Iggy the rest, recounting an oedipal dream he'd once had. There was slippage between what was Bowie's and what was Iggy's, and Bowie had played "Sister Midnight" a few times live on tour, but it eventually became the first cut on *The Idiot*, as well as the first real fruit of their fertile (and later not so fertile) partnership.

Bowie remained in Clos-des-Mésanges for most of June, working, painting and reading. He paid visits to Charlie Chaplin's wife, Oona, who lived nearby. ("This intelligent, very sensitive fellow who came from the same part of London as Charlie, walked in and wanted to talk. I really am very fond of him.") He was often seen out and about in local bars and restaurants, dressed simply and generally keeping his head down. But by the end of the month he'd had enough, and decamped with Iggy Pop back to the Château d'Hérouville.

The sixteenth century Château was a former coach staging post and stables, built in the ruins of a castle, and was said to be the setting for secret trysts between Frédéric Chopin and his lover George Sand. Its vast wings contained some thirty bedrooms, rehearsal rooms, kitchens, a dining hall and a gaming room. Outside there was a swimming pool, tennis courts, a beautiful complex of fountains and waterfalls and even a mini-castle, complete with its own moat. The grounds were enormous and one had the impression of being completely isolated and deep in the country-side, despite the fact that Paris was less than an hour away.

It was the first ever residential studio suite—a concept that was much copied afterwards. Two studios were located in outhouses, probably former stables, while a third was in the right wing. In 1976, it cost 5,500 francs (£550, $1,000) per day to hire a studio at the Château, not including tape, which was expensive back then (700 francs for a 50mm roll). Session musicians would get around 1,000 francs for a day's work. The studios were very state-of-the art for the era; the one Bowie used for *The Idiot* and *Low* had an MCI-500 console and the first Westlake monitors to be installed in Europe. Originally opened in 1969, the Château studios had taken a few years before building up an international reputation, which eventually came when Elton John recorded *Honky Château* there in 1972. Since then, the Château's ever-expanding clientèle counted the likes of Pink Floyd, the Grateful Dead, T-Rex, Rod Stewart, Bill Wyman, Cat Stevens and the Bee-Gees plus dozens of French artists.

Bowie and Iggy Pop settled in at the Château; their idea was to record when the mood took them, but to basically take it easy. On the face of it, they made for unlikely friends. Although there were certain things in common—both rock performers, both in something of a personal and artistic impasse, both struggling with drugs and mental health problems—it was basically a case of opposites attracting. Bowie was the sexually ambiguous English dandy; Iggy Pop the hyper-masculine American rocker. Career-wise, Bowie was riding a tidal wave, his fame largely transcending the rock world. By contrast, Iggy Pop was at an all-time low, flat broke, without a band and without a recording contract, until Bowie used his weight to get him one at RCA. Bowie was the consummate professional: even during the nightmare of his cocaine addiction, he still toured his albums, touted himself regularly in the media, starred in a movie and, of course, made records that many consider his finest. Iggy Pop, on the other hand, was erratic, disorganised, had no self-discipline, wouldn't turn up to studio sessions, hadn't put out a record in years—and was essentially heading for a massive fall without the helping hand of someone of Bowie's calibre.

It would seem that Iggy Pop needed Bowie a hell of a lot more than Bowie needed him. But Iggy had a certain underground cachet that Bowie probably envied. "I was not executive material like him," Iggy Pop said in 1996. "I couldn't do the things he seemed to do so well and so easily. Yet I knew I had something he didn't have and could never have." The Iggy persona was about danger and violence, urban edge, outlaw posturing, rawness, unrestrained liberty to the point of nihilism…in short, a blunt instrument of American masculinity, and the polar opposite of what Bowie was about at the time. "David always had a weakness for tough guys," was how his friend Marc Bolan bitchily put it. Likewise, Iggy Pop had been intrigued by the "British music-hall, pure vaudeville" quality he'd seen in Bowie the first time they'd met. In other words, it was a perfect match of alter egos.

There was a touch of Tom Ripley in the way Bowie adopted those he admired, as if they were another role to be played. Bowie had already sought out and befriended another American hard man, Lou Reed, in rather similar circumstances. Lou Reed's former band the Velvet Underground was of course a legendary nexus of the sixties New York scene, but by the early seventies Reed was down on his luck and in desperate need of a leg up. Enter David Bowie, who talked Reed up in the media and produced *Transformer* (1972)—which did indeed transform Reed's career through the classic hit "Walk on the Wild Side." The album is largely about New York's gay and transvestite scene, and the glammed-up Bowie certainly helped bring out Lou Reed's inner drag queen. In a sense, he did the same for Iggy Pop, suffusing Iggy's balls-out rock routine with a more ironic, cabaret sensibility, giving him a veneer of sleazy European sophistication.

For Bowie, *The Idiot* wasn't just about resurrecting Iggy Pop's stalled career. It was also a dry run for *Low*, with which it would be recorded almost back-to-back, in the same studios. In fact, the recordings overlapped. Sound engineer Laurent Thibault: "*Low* was recorded after *The Idiot*, but *Low* came out first. David didn't want people to think he'd been inspired by Iggy's album, when in fact it was all the same thing. There were even tracks that we recorded for Iggy that ended up on *Low*, such as 'What in the World,' which was originally called 'Isolation.' " (You can hear Iggy's backing vocals on "What in the World.") Bowie produced *The Idiot*, played many of the instruments and cowrote all the songs—the lyrics largely written by Iggy and the music by Bowie. "Poor Jim [Iggy's real name], in a way, became a guinea pig for what I wanted to do with sound," Bowie explained later. "I didn't have the material at the time, and I didn't feel like writing it all. I felt much more like laying back and getting behind someone else's work, so that album was opportune, creatively." Iggy Pop agrees: "[Bowie] has a work pattern that recurs again and again. If he has an idea about an area of work that he wants to enter, as a first step, he'll use side-projects or work for other people to gain experience and gain a little taste of water before he goes in and does his…and I think he used working with me that way also."

As with *Low*, the recording was all done at night, from around midnight on. Bowie covered keyboards, saxophone and most of the guitar parts; the other musicians were Michel Marie on drums and Laurent Thibault on bass. Phil Palmer, nephew of Kinks frontman Ray Davies, played guitar on "Nightclubbing," "Dum Dum Boys" and "China Girl." Carlos Alomar wasn't present, but the rest of Bowie's rhythm section (Dennis Davis and George Murray) turned up a few weeks in. According to Robert Fripp, Bowie had asked him and Eno to attend as well, but "it so happened that David and Iggy had a dispute and the project was post-poned." Keyboardist Edgar Froese of Tangerine Dream was also at the Château, but apparently had to leave before recording had got properly under way. And Ricky Gardiner, guitarist with prog rock group Beggar's Opera, had also orig-inally been asked to lend a hand on *The Idiot*, but "then I had this last-minute phone call saying that it was no longer nec-essary for me to go, and that Mr Bowie sent his apologies," he later recalled. A few weeks later, he got another call sum-moning him to the Château, "asking could I go off…and perform miracles on the new album?" That new album was of course *Low*.

In the studio, Iggy would sit writing lyrics on the studio floor, surrounded by books and piles of paper. But musical-ly, it was Bowie who was in control. He'd arrived with bits of instrumentals recorded on minicassettes, which he'd play to the musicians. The way he directed them was autistic to say the least: "I'd continually ask him if what we were play-ing was OK," recalled Laurent Thibault in 2002. "He would-n't reply. He'd just stare at me without saying a word. That was when I realised he was never going to reply. For exam-ple, Bowie would be playing a Baldwin piano hooked up to a Marshall amp. Michel gets up from his drumkit to see what Bowie's up to. Bowie still won't say a word. And I'm record-ing it all. David would listen back to the tape, and once he was happy with the results, we'd move on to the next thing. After a while, we stopped bothering to ask him anything."

They recorded quickly, without it ever being explicit whether they were working on Iggy's album or Bowie's.

According to Thibault, *Low*'s signature crashing drum sound was conceived in these sessions as well. The Château was the first in Europe to have an Eventide Harmonizer, which is an electronic pitch-shifting device—you could raise or lower the pitch of any instrument directly without having to slow the tape down, as had been previously necessary. Bowie apparently decided to hook the Harmonizer up to the drums, with astonishing results. This account doesn't really square with Visconti's, though (as we'll see a little later on). And listening to *The Idiot*, although it does seem that some songs have a treated drum sound (particularly "Funtime"), it's not nearly as evolved or as startling as what Visconti developed for *Low*.

At the time, Iggy Pop excitedly talked up *The Idiot* as a cross between Kraftwerk and James Brown. That's an exaggeration, and would actually be a better description of the first side of *Low*. *The Idiot* is still mostly a rock album—replete with heavy metal–style licks—and doesn't really play off a pop sensibility in the way *Low* does. But Bowie's genre-thieving, magpie sensibility makes itself felt. A funk feel creeps in on most tracks; synthesisers fill out the sound (sometimes mimicking strings, sometimes as sound effects); an early use of a drum machine features on "Nightclubbing"; and the dissonant, wandering lead guitar lines (mostly played by Bowie) are pretty similar to what Ricky Gardiner achieved on the first side of *Low*. The experimentalism is most apparent on the final track, "Mass Production," with its looped industrial noise. "We made a tape loop using David's ARP," recalled Laurent Thibault, "but it sounded too erratic and David didn't like it. So I had the idea of recording it on a quarter-inch tape, and once he was satisfied, I set up a loop so huge we had to set up mic stands right round the console. As the loop went round, you could see the little white joining tape, making it look like a toy train. David sat on his swivelling chair for three quarters of an hour, just watching the tape circle go round and round the four corners of the room, until finally he uttered the word 'record.'" (Of course, this was in the days before sequencers—nowadays you could do all that on a computer in a few minutes.)

The Idiot also finds Iggy Pop straining towards other idioms, experimenting with his voice: "To work with [Bowie] as a producer…he was a pain in the ass—megalomaniacal, loco! But he had good ideas. The best example I can give you was when I was working on the lyrics to 'Funtime' and he said, 'Yeah, the words are good. But don't sing it like a rock guy. Sing it like Mae West.' Which made it informed of other genres, like cinema. Also, it was a little bit gay. The vocals there became more menacing as a result of that suggestion."

Iggy's catatonic, lugubrious croon—like a drugged-up Frank Sinatra—is one of the signatures of the album. As on *Station to Station*, the crooning comes over as a form of alienated male hysteria. The emotionally skewed quality of the album is apparent right from the first track, the superb "Sister Midnight." A funk bass and riff play against dirty, dissonant guitars, while Iggy Pop's basso profundo contrasts weirdly with Bowie's falsetto yelps. The lyrics set the tormented, psychiatric tone of the album, as Iggy recounts a dream in which "Mother was in my bed, and I made love to her / Father he gunned for me, hunted me with his six-gun."

There's a relentlessly disturbing feel to the album that would be too much to take if it weren't for the camp touches and stabs of dark humour scattered across most of the tracks. The autistic worldview of *Low* is one in which relationships are an impossibility; on *The Idiot*, relationships are not only possible, they're a mutually destructive addiction. Songs kick off with a vision of happy codependence, only to sink into rupture and depression or violence. "China Girl" (reprised by Bowie six years later as a cheesy pop song, but excellent here) uses the analogy of East and West, as Iggy corrupts his oriental lover with "television, eyes of blue" and "men who want to rule the world." (The song also alludes to Bowie's messianic delusions: "I stumble into town, just like a sacred cow, visions of swastikas in my head, plans for everyone.") Even the jokey, cabaret-style "Tiny Girls" (a risqué title given Iggy Pop's sexual proclivities of the time) ends with the sour message of a world where even the " girls who have got no tricks" ultimately "sing of greed, like a young banshee." Relationships are power struggles in which lies and deception are the weapons, and the strong crush the weak.

There's misogyny, but also plenty of self-hate in there too—in fact it's pretty much the sort of album you'd expect two junkies running away from deteriorating relationships might make. But the songs are mostly leavened with irony and humorous touches. The exception is the eight and half minutes of the final track—nothing on the rest of the album matches the sheer nihilism of "Mass Production." (Eno described listening to the album as akin to sticking your head in concrete, which is not true at all, except perhaps for this one track.) Crunching, industrial synth sounds fight distorted guitars over the genocidal imagery of "smokestacks belching, breasts turn brown." Iggy Pop croons against the backdrop of suicide ("although I try to die, you put me back on the line"), begging the lover who thanklessly saved him to "give me the number of a girl almost like you," since "I'm almost like him." The estrangement from the self is now complete, and the song collapses in a morass of detuned synthesisers and grinding noise.

Bowie's stylistic *imprimatur* is all over the album. Even the title's literary allusion is more Bowie than Pop. The cover is a black-and-white shot of Iggy Pop in a karate-style pose inspired by the painting *Roquairol* by the German Expressionist painter Erich Heckel—a Bowie-esque reference. Not only did Bowie write most of the music, he also suggested song subjects and titles, and generally kick-started Iggy's imagination. For "Dum Dum Boys," "I only had a few notes on the piano, I couldn't quite finish the tune," Iggy Pop recounted later. "Bowie said, 'Don't you think you could do something with that? Why don't you tell the story of the Stooges?' He gave me the concept of the song and he also gave me the title. Then he added that guitar arpeggio that metal groups love today. He played it, and then he asked Phil Palmer to play the tune again because he didn't find his playing technically proficient enough." The danger of the album being perceived as Bowie's was something Iggy Pop was well aware of, and shaped his work on their following collaboration, *Lust for Life:* "The band and Bowie would leave the studio and go to sleep, but not me. I was working to be one step ahead of them for the next day… See, Bowie's a hell of a fast guy. Very quick thinker, quick action, very active person, very sharp. I realised I had to be quicker than him, otherwise whose album was it going to be?"

And yet, the influence was definitely not just a one-way street. The harsher, messier guitar sound is something that infused *Low* and was further developed on *"Heroes"*. Bowie was also particularly impressed with Iggy's way with words: "'[China Girl]' has an extraordinary lyric, and it was really sort of thrown out as he was writing it," Bowie recalled in 1993. "It was literally just thrown out on the recording session, almost verbatim. He changed maybe three or four lines. But it was an extraordinary talent that he had for spontaneous free thought."

Iggy Pop's lyrics pointed Bowie towards a new way to write, which shows up on *Low* ("the walls close in and I need some noise" ["Dum Dum Boys"] sounds a bit like a lost line from "Sound and Vision"). On previous albums, you got the feeling that Bowie's efforts to escape cliché had him resorting to ever more baroque constructions and *recherché* imagery. And sometimes, he went too far ("where the dogs decay defecating ecstasy, you're just an ally for the leecher, locator of the virgin king"). But with Iggy Pop, there's no sixth-form cleverness. He pulls off the trick of avoiding cliché while keeping it simple, direct and personal. Death stalks the seventies work of both Bowie and Iggy Pop, but Bowie has nothing quite so blunt as "though I try to die, you put me back on the line." Instead, he locates the death impulse in the mystique of rock 'n' roll suicides, of lovers jumping in the river holding hands, and so on. Such romantic imagery is eschewed on *Low*.

The Idiot is a blistering album that brought out the best in both of them. It was no great commercial success at the time, but then again no commercial concessions had been made in its creation either. Nonetheless, in its way, *The Idiot* turned out to be just as influential as *Low*. It's hard to imagine the curdled croon of Joy Division's Ian Curtis if Iggy Pop hadn't got there first. And "Mass Production" is almost a template for Joy Division (and quite probably the last song Ian Curtis ever heard as well—*The Idiot* was still spinning on the turntable when his wife discovered his lifeless body). If

Iggy Pop was the godfather of punk, then *The Idiot* was the sound of Iggy keeping a step ahead (with Bowie's help of course), shepherding a new generation towards the post-punk scene of the late seventies and early eighties.

Bowie was still suffering from mental problems—from paranoia and black magic delusions. On several occasions he'd turned up at the hospital at nearby Pontoise, convinced he was being poisoned. Another time, Iggy Pop playfully pushed him into the Château swimming pool. Visibly shaken, Bowie decided to abandon the recording sessions on the spot—months before at a party in Los Angeles, the actor Peter Sellers had warned him of the occult danger of "dark stains" at the bottom of swimming pools. The sessions were held up for several days, until Iggy persuaded him to return. Sound engineer Laurent Thibault also got on the wrong end of Bowie's paranoia. Thibault basically coproduced the album and comixed it as well, with Tony Visconti, but Bowie left him (and all session musicians) off the credits. Bowie had got it into his head that Thibault had smuggled a journalist into the Château, although in fact he'd known all about it and probably arranged it. "David wasn't there for the interview, but he told me a journalist was coming and told me what I had to say to him," recalled Thibault. "Then after, when David returned to the Château, he threw the copy of *Rock 'n' Folk* [a sort of French *Rolling Stone*] at my face as he got out of the car. He said he didn't know there was a traitor among us…. The journalist had asked the names of the musicians. David had been happy to share the information, but had changed his mind since, he didn't want anyone to know. He then told me that this French article might appear internationally, that what I'd said would be taken at face value, and that, consequently, he couldn't put my name on the record sleeve. Of course, my jaw dropped to the ground, and on the way back to Paris, he said that it'd teach me a lesson."

In August, with the Château already booked for another band, the *Idiot* sessions moved on to the Munich Musicland studios, owned by Giorgio Moroder. Bowie met up with Moroder and his producer partner Peter Bellote, the architects of the synthetic eurodisco sound that was sweeping Germany at the time. There were never any plans to work together at that time (they would do years later), but viewed from a certain angle, Moroder and Bowie weren't so very far apart in what they were doing. Moroder was using the New York disco sound and marrying it with synthesisers and a thumping robotic beat to create a particularly European-flavoured dance music. And the following year, Moroder and Bellote would produce Donna Summer's hugely influential synth disco anthem "I Feel Love," which impressed Eno greatly at the time.

According to Bowie, he and Eno started meeting up at around this point. Bowie: "At our regular sound swap-meets in 1976, Eno and I exchanged sounds that we loved. Eno offered, among others, his then current fave, Giorgio

Moroder and Donna Summer's military R&B and I played him Neu! and the rest of the Düsseldorf sound. They sort of became part of our soundtrack for the year." This sounds a little unlikely—Eno would have already heard Neu! by the summer of 1976, since he'd already met and worked with Neu! guitarist Michael Rother (Rother's other group, Harmonia, had been championed by Eno as early as 1974).

In any case, Neu! was certainly a part of Bowie's musical landscape at the time: "I bought my first vinyl *Neu! 2* in Berlin around 1975 while I was on a brief visit," he later recalled. "I bought it because I knew that they were a spin-off of Kraftwerk and had to be worth hearing. Indeed, they were to prove to be Kraftwerk's wayward, anarchistic brothers. I was completely seduced by the setting of the aggressive guitar-drone against the almost-but-not-quite robotic/machine drumming of Dinger. Although fairly tenuous, you can hear a little of their influence on the track *Station to Station*. Indeed, in the summer of '76 I called Michael Rother and asked whether he would be interested in working with myself and Brian Eno on my new album entitled *Low*. Although enthusiastic, Michael had to decline and to this day I wonder how that trilogy would have been affected by his input."

Again, Bowie is muddling a few things up here. He wasn't in Europe at any time in 1975, so presumably it was more like the spring of 1976 that he first got hold of a Neu! album. (That perplexes me, since I too detect a Neu! influence on *Station to Station*.) And Michael Rother recalls being contacted by Bowie in 1977 for the *"Heroes"* sessions, not for *Low*. According to a 2001 interview with Bowie in *Uncut* magazine, it was one "Michael Dinger" who had been Bowie's first choice for guitarist on *Low*. Bowie no doubt means Klaus Dinger, the other half of the Neu! duo. Bowie had supposedly called him up from the Château, but Dinger had politely refused.

Rother and Dinger had originally played in Kraftwerk, but left in 1971 to pursue their more organic sound, recording three influential albums (*Neu*, *Neu! 2* and *Neu! 75*). The Neu! sound was about textures, and about stripping things back to simple structures until you arrived at a spacey, meditative groove, often referred to as *motorik*. (Eno: "There were three great beats in the 70s: Fela Kuti's Afrobeat, James Brown's Funk and Klaus Dinger's Neu! beat.") *Motorik* was basically a steady 4/4 rhythm that would often fade in slowly, but what made it different was that there were no tempo changes, no syncopation and minimal variations. The guitars and other instrumentation accompanied the beat, rather than the other way around. It was very human, a pulse that simply went on and on, inducing a trancelike state of mind and the gentle welling of emotion. "It's a feeling, like a picture, like driving down a long road or lane," Klaus Dinger explained in 1998. "It is essentially about life, how you have to keep moving, get on and stay in motion."

Bowie mentions Neu! quite a bit at this time, but I don't

hear anything on *Low* that sounds too much like them (although "A New Career in a New Town" is something of a tribute to Neu! offshoot La Düsseldorf). Nonetheless, there is a convergence in the approach of bands like Neu! and what Bowie was to do on *Low*. The feeling that a lot of German artists had then of being forced to start again with a blank page after the betrayals of a previous generation, of having to pare it all down to nothing in order to see what will emerge, all that resonates on *Low*. The rock star moves and masks partially give way to a junky trying to kick the habit while living above an auto repair shop in an immigrant quarter of Berlin. "Nothing to say, nothing to do…I will sit right down, waiting for the gift of sound and vision."

Another element that the Bowie of *Low* shares with German bands like Neu! and Can is the willingness to treat music as soundscapes, rather than structured songs with their melodic "narratives." That very much informs tracks like "Weeping Wall" or "Subterraneans." These have an emotional quietude about them as well, quite different from the histrionic register that Bowie more often retreated to on earlier albums to express emotion. Many of the German bands also shared a strategy of radical repetition overlaid with experimentation. There was Neu!'s *motorik* rhythm, Kraftwerk's robotic beats, but also Can's endless grooves on songs like "Halleluwa," that sound like a long jam but were in fact carefully reconstructed in the studio with tape loops. Bowie and Eno were converging on similar studio-driven ideas of repetition-plus-experimentation.

From Munich, the *Idiot* sessions moved on to Berlin, and the Hansa-by-the-wall studios. The nucleus of the *Low* team assembled there for some final work on *The Idiot*—rhythm section Carlos Alomar, Dennis Davis and George Murray, as well as producer Tony Visconti, whom Bowie had called in to mix the *Idiot* tapes. He'd wanted Visconti to produce, but he hadn't been available, so Bowie had done the job himself aided by Laurent Thibault. Visconti found the tape quality to be fairly poor—a "salvage job"—and did the best he could with what he was given. (In retrospect, *The Idiot*'s slightly muddy sound adds to rather than detracts from the album.)

This was the first time Bowie had worked at Hansa-by-the-wall, where he and Visconti would later mix *Low* and then record its follow-up *"Heroes"*. The studio was only twenty or thirty metres from the Wall: "From the control room we could see the Wall and we could also see over the Wall and over the barbed wire to the Red Guards in their gun turrets," recalled Visconti of his time working at Hansa. "They had enormous binoculars and they would look into the control room and watch us work, because they were as star-struck as anyone. We asked the engineer one day whether he felt a bit uncomfortable with the guards staring at him all day. They could easily have shot us from the East, it was that close. With a good telescopic sight, they could have put us out. He said you get used to it after a while and then he turned, took an overhead light and pointed it at the guards, sticking his tongue out and jumping up and down generally hassling them. David and I just dived right under the recording desk. 'Don't do that,' we said because we were scared to death!"

It was the charged, John Le Carré aspect of Berlin as it was then. "The thing about all those Bowie/Eno/Iggy/Hansa albums was the mythology that went with their creation," mused New Order drummer Stephen Morris in 2001. "Why was a studio overlooking the Berlin Wall so important?" The Wall provided almost too much symbolism for one city to bear. All cities construct myths around themselves—but in the Berlin of the sixties and seventies, the myth was in danger of smothering the city under it. This was Berlin as the decadent outpost of the West—dangerously cut off and etiolated, frozen in the aftermath of disaster, a city that continued to pay for its sins, where paranoia was not a sign of madness but the correct response to the situation. The symbolism of the Wall was as much psychological as it was political. Not only was it a microcosm of the Cold War, it was also a mirror you could gaze into and see a looking-glass world, utterly like yours but utterly different as well. It divided mentalities, and expanded schizophrenia to the size of a city. And the Wall was just one of many layers of the myth of Berlin.

waiting for the gift

With *The Idiot* mixed, Bowie retreated to his home in Switzerland, where Eno shortly joined him. Together they started writing and throwing around ideas for the new album, then provisionally called *New Music: Night and Day* (a title that caught the concept of the two different sides, but which sounded rather pompously like the work of a minimalist composer). A few weeks before the sessions got under way, Bowie had put in a call to Visconti: "He phoned me up, it was actually a conference call, he had Brian on one line, himself on another," Visconti later told Australian broadcaster Allan Calleja. "I was in London, and David and Brian were in Switzerland I think, where David used to live. David said: 'We have this conceptual album here, we want to make it really different, we're writing these strange songs, these very short songs.' It was conceived right from the beginning that one side was going to be pop songs and the other side was going to be ambient music in the style of Brian and Tangerine Dream and Kraftwerk." Actually, it seemed that the original idea had been not so much pop songs for the first side but raw rock songs, with minimal studio intervention. That would have emphasised two completely different approaches, probably at the expense of any sonic unity at all. But perhaps Bowie had got the raw rock idea out of his system with *The Idiot*, and working with Eno was always going to be more about pop.

The idea was radical experimentation. Visconti again: "The three of us agreed to record with no promise that *Low* would ever be released. David had asked me if I didn't mind wasting a month of my life on this experiment if it didn't go well. Hey, we were in a French château for the month of September and the weather was great!" Bowie asked Visconti what he thought he could contribute to the sessions; Visconti mentioned the pitch-shifting Eventide Harmonizer he'd just got. Bowie asked what it did, and Visconti famously replied that "it fucks with the fabric of time!" Bowie was delighted, and "Eno went berserk. He said: 'We've got to have it!' "

Brooklyn-born, Tony Visconti had started out playing in various bands in New York and elsewhere across the country, carving out a reputation on the circuit as a proficient bass player and guitarist. He'd put out a couple of singles as part of a duo with his wife Siegrid, but when the last single flopped he took up a job as a house producer with a New

York label. Shortly after, he relocated to London, where he met a not-yet-successful David Bowie at the early stages of his career. Together they recorded *Space Oddity* (excluding the title track) and *The Man Who Sold the World*, although Visconti missed out on the albums that propelled Bowie into bona fide rock stardom (*Ziggy Stardust*, *Aladdin Sane*). But he'd hooked up with Bowie again to mix *Diamond Dogs* and produce *Young Americans*, Bowie's first smash hit in the States.

Visconti had come of age as a producer in late sixties London, a crossover period where producers were becoming a lot less like lab technicians and more like an invisible member of the band, the one with a handle on the technology that would drive experimentation. George Martin's mid-sixties work with the Beatles was clearly one kind of template for Visconti. Instead of the live takes of the early Beatles albums, Martin would take different instrumental, vocal and percussion tracks and build them up, layer upon layer, over a number of sessions. In other words, the process started having a more direct influence on the content. Visconti has singled out "Strawberry Fields" as the moment where "George showed us once and for all that the recording studio itself was a musical instrument." The Beatles had recorded two versions of the song, one more psychedelic, and one more understated, with classically inspired instrumentation. Lennon liked the beginning of the first and the end of the second; the trouble was they were recorded at slightly different speeds, and the keys differed by a semitone. Martin speeded up one version, slowed down the other, then spliced the two together. "This track was the dividing line of those who recorded more or less live and those who wanted to take recorded music to the extremes of creativity," Visconti later commented to *Billboard*. Here, you can already see the intersection of Visconti's and Eno's vision of the studio, even if they're converging from different standpoints.

The fact that Visconti hadn't come up through the ranks at a studio but had started off as a musician also gave him a different, more hybrid take on the duties of a producer. He could play several instruments, and was excellent at arrangements. It was another area where he had at first looked to George Martin: "I would read Beethoven and Mozart and learn the voicings from how they voiced the string section, and I'd apply that. And then I'd listen to George Martin, and I'd say, 'That's what he did. He listened to Bach....' He's taking something classical and old and tried and true and putting it in a pop context, so I just worked it out. And I just imitated him for a few years until I developed some tricks of my own." All this cross-disciplinary expertise meant that Visconti tended to play a greater role in the studio than most producers. On Bowie albums, Visconti is not only sound engineer and mixer, but often scores the arrangements (the cello part on "Art Decade," for instance), and sometimes sings and plays various instruments as well.

The *Low* sessions kicked off at the Château on September 1st, without Eno for the first few days. The assembled band was the R&B rhythm section Bowie had had since *Young Americans*, namely Carlos Alomar, George Murray and Dennis Davis. On lead guitar was Ricky Gardiner, a suggestion of Visconti's, after Bowie's other choices had fallen through (Visconti and Gardiner had been working on demos for what would become Visconti's only solo album, *Inventory*). The main keyboardist was Roy Young, formerly of the Rebel Rousers; he'd also played with the Beatles in the early sixties. Young had first met Bowie in 1972 when they'd played on the same bill; Bowie had wanted him for *Station to Station*, but had given him too short notice. Then, in the summer of '76, Young had been playing in London when Bowie had called him from Berlin, asking him to come over. Apparently Bowie had originally wanted to do *Low* at Hansa, but then changed his mind, probably because he'd already paid upfront for studio time in France. In any case, a few days later he called Young again to switch the venue to the Château.

Bowie's and Visconti's working methods crystallised on the *Low* sessions. They would start late. (Eno: "It was all overnight, so I was in a kind of daze a lot of the time, days drifting into one another.") As with *The Idiot*, Bowie came into the studio with various bits and pieces on tape—*The Man Who Fell to Earth* material; leftovers from the *Idiot* sessions; stuff he'd recorded at his home in Switzerland—but no complete songs written, and no lyrics. In other words, the studio was very much part of the writing process. To begin with, the rhythm section would be told to jam with a loose chord progression. There might be minimal direction from Bowie or Visconti, and some experimenting with different styles, but basically they'd simply keep kicking the progression around until something emerged that developed into an arrangement. Carlos Alomar: "I'd get together with the drummer and the bass player and we'd work on a song, maybe reggae, maybe slow or fast or up-tempo, and we'd let David hear it three or four different ways, and whichever way he wanted to do it, we just did it.... Basically he says: 'How about something like this?' 'OK fine.' I just start grooving and start playing until I came up with something, and that ability has been like the saving grace." The rhythm section provided the seed bed for most of the first side, and Bowie was generous with writing credits if he thought one of the musicians had come up with a defining element of the song. Alomar already had credits for his riffs on "Fame" and "Sister Midnight." On *Low*, Bowie cut credits for "Breaking Glass" three ways with bass player George Murray and drummer Dennis Davis.

This initial backing-track phase was very quick and in the case of *Low* took only five days, after which Dennis Davis and George Murray played no further part in the proceedings (in fact, by the time Eno turned up at the Château, they'd already left). Once Bowie was happy with the backing tracks, work with the overdubs could begin—essentially recording guitar and other solos. Alomar would normally have come up with an initial solo to hold the rhythm section together, but then record a new one later. Ricky Gardiner and Roy Young would be recording their parts too. On *Low*, these were generally further electronically treated by Visconti, Eno or Bowie (there's not a lot of "natural" sound on *Low*), so this is where the sessions would enter a more experimental, nebulous phase. Some of it was about treating instruments as the musicians were playing, with Visconti using the Harmonizer, various tone filters, reverbs and a panoply of other studio tricks.

Eno would mostly be using a portable synth he'd brought along with him. Visconti: "He has an old synthesiser that fits into a briefcase made by a defunct company called EMS. It didn't have a piano keyboard like modern synths. It did have a lot of little knobs, a peg board and little pegs, like an old telephone switch board to connect the various parameters to one another. But its *pièce de résistance* was a little 'joystick' that you find on arcade games. He would pan that joystick around in circles and make swirling sounds." (This synth lives on, and Bowie even used it on a recent album, *Heathen*: "Some years ago, a friend very kindly bought me the original EMS AKS briefcase synth that Eno used on so many of those classic records of the seventies. In fact, it was the one he used on *Low* and *"Heroes"*. It was up for auction, and I got it for my fiftieth birthday....

Taking it through customs has always been a stomach-turning affair as it looks like a briefcase bomb in the x-ray. Eno got pulled out of the line on several occasions. I wouldn't even dream of taking it through these days.'')

This was also the phase where Eno would often be left alone in the studio to lay down a "sonic bed." Eno: "I was trying to give some kind of sonic character to the track so that the thing had a distinct textural feel that gave it a mood to begin with.... It's hard to describe that because it was never the same twice, and it's not susceptible to description very easily in ordinary musical terms. It would just be doing the thing that you can do with tape so that you can treat the music as malleable. You have something down there but then you can start squeezing it around and changing the colour of this and putting this thing much further in front of something else and so on."

Where the rhythm section was about finding the groove that worked—in other words, locating the pattern—Eno was more concerned with breaking those patterns that the mind instinctively slotted into, when left to its own devices. One of the methods that he and Bowie used on *Low* was the "Oblique Strategies" he'd created with artist Peter Schmidt the year before. It was a deck of cards, and each card was inscribed with a command or an observation. When you got into a creative impasse, you were to turn up one of the cards and act upon it. The commands went from the sweetly banal ("Do the washing up") to the more technical ("Feedback recordings into an acoustic situation"; "The tape is now the music"). Some cards contradict each other ("Remove specifics and convert to ambiguities"; "Remove ambiguities and convert to specifics"). Some use Wildean substitution ("Don't be afraid of things because they're easy to do"). And several veer towards the Freudian ("Your mistake was a hidden intention"; "Emphasise the flaws"). The stress is on capitalising on error as a way of drawing in randomness, tricking yourself into an interesting situation, and crucially leaving room for the thing that can't be explained—an element that every work of art needs.

Did the Oblique Strategy cards actually work? They were probably more important symbolically than practically. A cerebral theoretician like Eno had more need of a mental circuit-breaker than someone like Bowie, who was a natural improviser, *collagiste*, artistic gadfly. Anyone involved in the creative arts knows that chance events in the process play an important role, but to my mind there's something slightly self-defeating about the idea of "planned accidents." Oblique Strategies certainly created tensions, as Carlos Alomar explained to Bowie biographer David Buckley: "Brian Eno had come in with all these cards that he had made and they were supposed to eliminate a block. Now, you've got to understand something. I'm a musician. I've studied music theory, I've studied counterpoint and I'm used to working with musicians who can read music. Here comes Brian Eno and he goes to a blackboard. He says: 'Here's the beat, and when I point to a chord, you play the chord.' So we get a random picking of chords. I finally had to say, 'This is bullshit, this sucks, this sounds stupid.' I totally, totally resisted it. David and Brian were two intellectual guys and they had a very different camaraderie, a heavier conversation, a Europeanness. It was too heavy for me. He and Brian would get off on talking about music in terms of history and I'd think, 'Well that's stupid—history isn't going to give you a hook for the song!' I'm interested in what's commercial, what's funky and what's going to make people dance!" It may well have been the creative tension between that kind of traditionalist approach and Eno's experimentalism that was more productive than the "planned accidents" themselves. As Eno himself has said: "The interesting place is not chaos, and it's not total coherence. It's somewhere on the cusp of those two."

The final stage of the recording would be the actual generation of a song. Bowie would experiment in front of the microphone, trying out different voices with different emotive qualities, eventually finding the one that would fit the song. There would be suggestions from Visconti and Eno, but this phase was more uniquely Bowie's show than any other's. Once he'd found the voice, the rest would slip into place—a melody line would materialise; the lyrics would find their shape. Some songs ("Sound and Vision," "Always Crashing in the Same Car") had extra verses, but when Bowie listened back he decided he didn't like them and they got wiped. In a way, he was doing everything backwards: nailing the context first, and finding the content afterwards. And ultimately, the lyric was as much texture as voice into-nation or instrumental background—to the point that the words in "Warszawa" are literally in an imaginary language, the semantic content bleached right out of the lyric.

through morning's thoughts

Low kicks off with a brief ode to movement, "Speed of Life." The difference between this opener and that of Bowie's previous album could hardly be more striking. As we've seen, *Station to Station*'s title track is a sweeping epic of cocaine romance. Although it has no narrative in the storybook sense, there is nonetheless a lyric arc that moves from the alienated magician "lost in my circle," to redemption in the "European canon." There is a musical arc too, with a succession of melody lines and a progression of themes. By contrast, "Speed of Life" is an instrumental—Bowie's first ever—and so has no narrative to offer. (Originally it was supposed to have lyrics, as was "A New Career in a New Town," but Bowie struggled to come up with the words on *Low*, and in the end these two pieces were left as they were.) Musically, it is not structured progressively, but cyclically (major theme repeated four times, bridge, minor theme repeated twice, major theme repeated four times, bridge, etc.). "Station" was a series of fragments spliced together and stretched out to breaking point. But "Speed of Life" is a fragment in isolation—as are most of the tracks on side one. (Eno: "He arrived with all these strange pieces, long and short, which already had their own form and structure. The idea was to work together to give the songs a more normal structure. I told him not to change them, to leave them in their bizarre, abnormal state.")

Like "Station to Station," "Speed of Life" fades in. But whereas "Station" has a train slowly coming in over the horizon, the fade-in to "Speed of Life" is abrupt, as if you'd arrived late and opened the door on a band in session. The album has already started without you! And that sense of catch-up never lets up on the track, which drives frenetically on until fade-out. It feels a little like one of the instrumentals from Eno's *Another Green World*, only re-recorded by someone in the manic phase of bipolar disorder.

The first thing you notice is the startling drum crash, like a fist pounding at your speaker. "When it came out, I thought *Low* was the sound of the future," recalled Joy Division/New Order drummer Stephen Morris. "When recording the *Ideal for Living* LP, I remember we kept asking the engineer to make the drums sound like 'Speed of Life'— strangely enough he couldn't." It was a trick Visconti used with the Eventide Harmonizer. He sent the snare to the

Harmonizer, which dropped the pitch, then fed it straight back to the drummer. It was done live, so Dennis Davis was hearing the distortion as he played, and responding accordingly. Visconti added the two onto the mix to get *Low*'s signature sound, which is not just the thump but also a descending echo. Visconti: "When the album came out the Harmonizer still wasn't widely available. I had loads of producers phoning me and asking what I had done, but I wouldn't tell them. I asked, instead, how they thought I did it and I got some great answers that I found inspirational. One producer insisted I compressed the drum tracks three separate times and slowed the tape down every time, or something like that." The heavily treated drums and the foregrounding of the bass was another inversion—instead of just getting the bass and drums down and doing the creative stuff on top, Visconti and Bowie were refocusing on the rhythm, which goes to the heart of what popular music is about. The sound itself later became a post-punk trope when producers finally twigged to how it was done, but at the time it was a radical departure.

Sonically, the first side of *Low* is about things opposing each other—the synthetic versus the organic, noise versus music, the abrasive versus the melodic. And it's all already there on "Speed of Life." The first sounds are the fade-in of a scratchy, descending dissonant synth noise—vaguely reminiscent of the one in "Mass Production"—which then plays over the swirling guitar and ARP arpeggios that make up the main theme (actually recycled from the intro of Bowie's novelty non-hit "The Laughing Gnome," from his wannabe light entertainer days). Everything is descending on this track: treated drums, lead guitar, synth effects, harmonising synths. And all the different elements are fighting it out, aggressively drawing attention to themselves as if in an orchestra composed of soloists. This is an album where the seams show: no bones are made about processed quality of the sound, which refuses to cohere in the way it did on *Station to Station*. Essentially, it's an artier take on *Station*'s funk-krautrock hybrid.

Just at the moment you might expect the track to develop into something else, or for the vocal to finally materialise (as it did after "Station to Station's" extended intro), "Speed of Life" fades out. It's a matter of deflecting expectations. Eno again: "What I think he was trying to do was to duck the momentum of a successful career. The main problem with success is that it has a huge momentum. It's like you've got this big train behind you and it wants you to carry on going the same way. Nobody wants you to step off the tracks and start looking round in the scrub around the edges because nobody can see anything promising there."

i'll never touch you

We have to wait for the second track before we get any Bowie vocals. "Breaking Glass" is another fragment, not even making two minutes, and probably the shortest song Bowie has ever recorded. It's got the heavily treated funk-disco beat, Eno's moog fanning from right to left speaker, and a menacing Carlos Alomar rock riff—one of the few stabs at a rock sensibility on the album. According to Alomar, "Dennis Davis had a lot to do with that. David wanted a song that was much lighter and much sillier, and 'Breaking Glass' was definitely it. If you leave a hole open in the music, you're going to get a signature line on the guitar for the introduction, which I duly did. For the rest of the song, I wanted to ape a Jew's harp, just a drone. We were just having fun. If you listen to all the quirks in the music—the call and response stuff between bass, guitar and drums—that was done with just three members of the band."

The last time we heard Bowie singing on record, on the final track of *Station to Station*, he was offering a seriously histrionic reading of the Tiomkin/Washington song "Wild Is the Wind." Bowie's neurotic croon on *Station to Station*—which owed more than a passing debt to Scott Walker—cranked up the drama value another few notches, adding to the weirdly tense atmosphere of that album. In complete contrast, Bowie comes over flat and monotone on "Breaking Glass." The alienation is still very much to the forefront, but it's no longer romantically overwrought. It's withdrawn and autistic. (One of the curious things about the album is how it surrenders what look like Bowie's strong points: his voice and his lyrics.) Iggy Pop's deadpan delivery on *The Idiot* is probably something of an influence, but in any case Bowie escapes the exaggerated vocal stylings that had characterised his work to date.

The lyric is also a fragment. There's no verse and chorus, just a few lines sung flatly, with a weirdly random emphasis on certain words ("Baby, I've BEEN breaking glass in your ROOM again / Don't look at the CARPET, I drew something AWFUL-ON-IT"). And there's no baroque imagery, no throwing darts in lovers' eyes. Alomar is not wrong to say that "Breaking Glass" is the light, silly song of the album, because there is something comic about the lyric, something of the child who knows he's been naughty. But there's also something creepily psycho about it, and the tension between the two is what makes it work.

In "What in the World" and "Sound and Vision," the bedroom is where we retreat to, to shut the world out. But the room in "Breaking Glass" is an altogether darker place. It's the locus of occult ritual. The track's title is most probably an occult allusion, and drawing "something awful" on the carpet certainly is. "Well, it is a contrived image, yes," Bowie said in 2001. "It refers to both the kabbalistic drawings of the Tree of Life and the conjuring of spirits." The single-line "Listen" and "See" are also strangely incantatory (as well as presaging "Sound and Vision"). Is Bowie commenting on the doomy, fetishised existence he'd led in Los Angeles? Or are the magical obsessions still current? Probably a bit of both. Although LA marked the highpoint of his cocaine psychosis and related occult fixations, they subsisted, and it was years before he could entirely shake them off. Throughout 1977 and 1978, the letters he would send friends and associates were marked with special numbers, to which he would ascribe occult meanings. While recording *Low*, he refused to sleep in the Château's master bedroom on the grounds that it was haunted. (And he seemed to persuade the others that it was too. Visconti: "The talk every night seemed to be about the ghosts that haunt the place.") Paranoia was a constant problem in his working relationships, to the point that even close collaborators like Visconti could come under suspicion. The hallucinations, too, persisted. "For the first two or three years afterward, while I was living in Berlin, I would have days where things were moving in the room," Bowie later recalled, "and this was when I was totally straight."

The lyric seems to have been composed in cut-up Burroughs fashion, where Bowie would take phrases he'd written and rearrange them in disorientating ways, trying to break down the sense for new meanings to emerge—or to cancel each other out. "Don't look" is followed by "See"; and "You're such a wonderful person" is followed by "But you got problems, I'll never touch you." The lyric is like a conversational fragment in which a psychotic who has just trashed his girlfriend's room is telling her that *she's* the mad one. It's a solipsistic world in which the psychosis is projected onto the other. The lyrics and intonation are without affect, without angst or self-awareness; we're seeing the psychosis from the inside.

That solipsism seems to me to be one of the psychological keys to the album. Everything becomes a reflection of the self, until you lose sight of where the self stops and the world begins. The instrumentals of the second side are tone poems that are ostensibly about places—Warsaw and Berlin. But they're really interior landscapes, extrapolating the world from the self. And that whole dialectic of objectivity and subjectivity informs the German Expressionist painters of the Die Brücke and Neue Sachlichkeit movements that Bowie was so keen on at around that time (of whom more later). Bowie once said that the work of the Die Brücke artists gave him the feeling that they were "describing something just as it was disappearing." That could aptly be applied to most of the songs on the first half of *Low*. Like "Speed of Life," "Breaking Glass" fades out just as the riff is starting to sink in. Just at the moment you think it might be leading somewhere, it's gone. According to Visconti, Bowie "couldn't come up with any lyrics when he was doing the music and thus that's why everything seems to fade." It was a case of making a virtue out of failure, out of running into a wall.

Through the occult allusions, "Breaking Glass" thematically links back to *Station to Station*. And the two albums, *Station to Station* and *Low*, are like the positive and negative symptoms of schizophrenia. *Station* is weird Crowley-esque mythology, girlfriends who disappear into the TV set and talking to God—it's a loghorreic stew of exaggeration, simmering hysteria and delusion. And *Low* is the other side of the psychosis. It's an autistic world of isolation and withdrawal, fragmentary thinking and mood swing, alogia and affective flattening…"I'll never touch you."

je est un autre

But it would be way too reductive to suggest that Bowie made a schizophrenic album because he was schizophrenic. The connections are a little more interesting than that. Bowie certainly drugged himself into a state in which schizophrenic-like behaviour emerged, although even through the worst of it he never totally spun out of orbit, as his professionalism and work rate testify. There's a part of his drug addiction that falls into cliché. After all, Bowie was hardly the only rock star in mid-seventies LA burning himself out on cocaine. Each era has its drug which translates its myth—in the mid-sixties, LSD reflected a naïve optimism about the possibility of change; and in the mid-seventies, cocaine echoed the grandiose nihilism of post-Manson LA. And Bowie fell into that trap.

Above and beyond all that, Bowie had long had a fascination with and horror of madness. It had informed most of his work to date, *The Man Who Sold the World* in particular. In the mid-seventies, Bowie often talked about the strain of madness that ran through his family, and his fear of inheriting it. His half-brother, Terry Burns, really was a schizophrenic. Terry was nine years older, and someone Bowie clearly looked up to as he was growing up. "It was Terry who started everything for me" he has said; their relationship was "extremely close." His brother was also artistically inclined (as many schizophrenics are), and acted as a mentor to Bowie, introducing him to jazz and rock, suggesting books to read—including Burroughs and Kerouac, with their Beat message of enlightenment through excess. Bowie's interest in Buddhism, which can perhaps be felt on *Low*, was also initially triggered by his brother. Terry's schizophrenia developed in the mid-sixties and he spent most of the rest of his life institutionalised. Bowie visited him at the Cane Hill psychiatric hospital in 1982, after which Terry developed a fixation on him, convinced that Bowie would return to rescue him. They didn't meet again, and Terry committed suicide in 1985. Bowie's 1970 track "All the Madmen" and his 1993 single "Jump They Say" are both about Terry, as is "The Bewlay Brothers" (1971) in all likelihood.

Bowie's interest in schizophrenia goes beyond the fact that his half-brother had the illness. At around this time Bowie was enthusiastically reading Julian Jaynes's *The Origin of Consciousness in the Breakdown of the Bicameral Mind*, a work that posits the essential schizophrenic nature of prehistoric man, and man's religious impulse as a direct result of it. Bowie has also had an abiding interest in "outsider art"—art produced by people with mental illness (hence the title of the nineties Bowie-Eno collaboration *Outside*). While making the Berlin trilogy, he and Eno visited Gugging, an Austrian psychiatric hospital-cum-art studio that encourages patients to paint. What Bowie derived from the experience was the artists' lack of self-consciousness. "None of them knew they were artists," he told journalist Tim de Lisle in 1995. "It's compelling and sometimes quite frightening to see this honesty. There's no awareness of embarrassment."

The subtext seems to be about regaining lost innocence through new ways of expression, unshackled by the conventions of "normal" society. Bowie's outsider art enthusiasm is reminiscent of the appropriation of primitive art by early 20th century modernists like Picasso. And to me there is something distinctly modernist about the schizophrenic world—in the alienation, the affectlessness, the fragmentation, the form over content, the hyper-subjectivity. There are clear similarities between the wordplay and disjointedness of modernist literature and schizophrenic discourse (the psychiatrist of James Joyce's schizophrenic daughter Lucia is reputed to have told him that the difference between the two was that "you dived to the bottom of the pool; she sank"). That wordplay is all over the songs of the schizophrenic Syd Barrett—a significant influence on Bowie—

reaching the highwater mark with his haunting "Word Song," which literally is just a jumble of alliterative words strung together. Bowie's cut-up writing style, derived from William S. Burroughs (yet another diagnosed schizophrenic), often has a similar feel to it, where the lyrics become a game of association and alliteration to the point of abstraction.

Schizophrenia stretches the personality in both directions. The schizophrenic is both less of a person and more of a person. Negative symptoms send him to a grey limbo of autistic disconnection; positive symptoms overstimulate the imagination, leading to a conflation of myth and reality. Since art is myth and performance is exaggeration, it's not too hard to draw the parallels. The rock celebrity world in particular is one of myth and fantasy, where behaviour that might normally be thought strange can be written off as just another personality trait. There aren't the same social brakes as in the "real" world. And all the more so for Bowie, whose coping strategy was to hive off characters that were fantasies of himself. But performance as therapy can be dangerous. Invented characters can take on a life of their own; masks and faces blur into one. The strategies used to avoid madness might ultimately be the ones that bring it on—eventually turning you into the thing you're fleeing from.

a little girl with grey eyes

Back to *Low*, and on to the third track, "What in the World"—according to Laurent Thibault a hold-over from the *Idiot* sessions. Clocking in at 2:23, it's barely any longer than "Breaking Glass." In a way, it's a composite of the two tracks that preceded it. Sonically, the cool rock menace of "Breaking Glass" is replaced with the compressed, synthetic frenzy of "Speed of Life," while lyrically the song plays the same game of projecting alienation on to another. If it's another fragment with no real verse/chorus structure, it nonetheless sounds a little more rounded than "Breaking Glass," less circular than "Speed of Life."

We're back with the crashing drums (with an even more pronounced disco flavour), while texturally, there's a synth-generated bubbling noise right up in the mix, sounding as though something's just about to boil over. Carlos Alomar's rhythm guitar has a soft, jazzy feel to it, jarring with Ricky

Gardiner's scratchy, neurotic lead work. The lead sounds eerily like Robert Fripp here, although he wasn't present at the *Low* sessions according to Bowie. But that messy, drunken guitar line (played elsewhere by Fripp) is a signature of Bowie albums from *Low* through to *Scary Monsters*.

Everything sounds speeded up—there's a building, manic quality to the song that is like the euphoric upswing of bipolar disorder. Bowie's voice remains flat and unengaged, and breaks down into a disturbing, wordless drone by the end of the song. The lyric is another cut-up jumble, with its juxtapositions of contradictory images, its meanings left behind in the hidden and unsaid. It's addressed to another girl with "problems": she's a reflection of the protagonist— withdrawn ("deep in your room, you never leave your room"), silent ("never mind, say something"), affectless ("love won't make you cry"). There's the disconnection of the previous song, from both the supposed interlocutor ("I'm just a little bit afraid of you") and from the self ("what you gonna say to the real me").

Bowie has said that at this period, "I was at the end of my tether physically and emotionally and had serious doubts about my sanity," but that "overall, I get a sense of real optimism through the veils of despair from *Low*. I can hear myself really struggling to get well." And perhaps you catch glimpses of that struggle in "What in the World." If it's impossible to take a lyric like "I'm in the mood for your love" at face value—it's too much of a rock cliché, especially with Bowie singing it in ironic rock mode—there might be something more mixed up and heartfelt in the "something deep inside of me, yearning deep inside of me, talking through the gloom."

nothing to do, nothing to say

In retrospect, it seems strange that an album like *Low* could have singles culled from it, but it had two, one of which was a sizeable hit in the UK, reaching number three (although it failed to make much impression on the other side of the Atlantic). Fractionally over three minutes long, "Sound and Vision" is at least the perfect length for a single, and it's also the song that most plays off a pop sensibility. The resemblances with a conventional pop hit of the time stop there, though. For a start, the intro is actually longer than the body of the song. It's almost like an instrumental with a lyric fragment tacked on at the end as an afterthought. "Sound and Vision" was the first song Bowie wrote at the Château specifically with Eno in mind, and this holding back of the vocals was Eno's idea, in order to create tension. It also returns us to lyric restraint after the garrulousness (by *Low*'s standards) of "What in the World."

On top of the Harmonized drums you can hear a hissing noise (actually a heavily gated snare), sitting strangely with a jaunty, jangly rhythm guitar riff and some synth melody lines that veer towards the cheesy. The "doo-doo" backing vocals, by Eno and Visconti's then wife Mary Hopkin (of "Those Were the Days" fame), add to the pastichey, ironic feel to the track: "I was out in France when they were recording *Low* and Brian Eno was there doing all the basic tracks for David to write songs around," Mary Hopkin later recalled. "Brian asked me to do some backing vocals with him, just a little riff. He promised me it'd be way back in the mix with tons of echo, but when David heard it he boosted it right up and it's very prominent, much to our embarrassment because it was such a corny little riff!" The sonic effect is that of a pop song with quotation marks, not quite sure whether it's a part of the genre or merely referencing it.

The backing vocals and instrumentation were "all recorded before there was even a lyric, title or melody," says Visconti. And the lyrics, when they finally did come, played against the skewed yet chipper concoction Eno had dreamed up. "Sound and Vision" was "the ultimate retreat song," according to Bowie. "It was just the idea of getting out of America, that depressing era I was going through. I was going through dreadful times. It was wanting to be put in a little cold room with omnipotent blue on the walls and blinds on the windows." The song is at the literal and thematic centre of the first side. After failing to connect with female others in "Breaking Glass" and "What in the World," the lyrics here are addressed only to the self, "drifting into my solitude," presaging the wordless, inward turn of the second side.

Bowie's transformations of the seventies were progressive stages of escape. *Ziggy Stardust* was a very English sort of Houdini act, slipping free from the dour constrictions of lower-middle-class life; from the suburbs; from England; and most of all from the self. *Low*'s key image of the room as refuge symbolises that other kind of escape, striking out for the interior, like Thomas Jerome Newton's "astronaut of inner space," and calling to mind Dostoevsky's dictum that "Life is in ourselves, and not in the external." The neurotic travel ("I've lived all over the world, I've left every place") is exchanged for the blankness of immobility.

"That's the colour of my room, where I will live": it's a room in a new town, Berlin, to which Bowie would move near the end of the *Low* sessions. Not a mansion with a swimming pool, but a first-floor flat in a slightly run-down building, in an immigrant area of a city of ghosts. After the razzle of glam rock, after the constant reinventions, the gaudy theatre of Ziggy Stardust or the Thin White Duke, it was something of a shock that Bowie could turn around and make an album that was so empty and private, with lyrics so sparse and simple, with "nothing to do, nothing to say." An album of waiting, of seeming nihilism. That shock and surprise is pretty evident in the music reviews of the day (which now come over as rather hysterical in themselves). In the *NME*, for instance, Charles Shaar Murray was writing about an album "so negative it doesn't even contain emptiness or the void," an album that is "futility and death-wish glorified, an elaborate embalming job for a suicide's grave."

That's to ignore the fact that there had always been a heavy dose of nihilism in most of Bowie's work—whether in his Nietzchean mode (*The Man Who Sold the World*), or in the gothic romances of doomed rock messiahs and Orwellian dystopias. Hedonism in the face of impending doom is a constant theme, reaching its elegiac peak in the title track of *Aladdin Sane*. Even the mostly euphoric *Young Americans* has a nihilistic undercurrent; the album is "the squashed remains of ethnic music as it survives in the age of Muzak rock, written and sung by a white limey," Bowie told Cameron Crowe in 1976. After all those rock star games, there was perhaps something liberating about declaring the essential emptiness of things—a declaration that may be related to Bowie's Buddhist enthusiasms of the 1960s.

That's not to say that Bowie was totally through with star games. Throughout the album, irony and sincerity are confused and blended. A creepy song like "Breaking Glass" has a jokey edge; "Sound and Vision" is both pop pastiche and an existential portrait; we're not quite sure whether to take the anguished entreaties of "Be My Wife" seriously or not. More to the point, we're not sure whether even Bowie is sure. He's the unreliable narrator, performing an eternal balancing act between sincerity and irony, even in the midst of personal crisis. His angst is at once genuine, and a modish pose. After all, "Bowie in Berlin"—with the studio by the Wall, escapades with partner-in-crime Iggy Pop, the Expressionist paintings, the Isherwood-ish life of decadence and dilettantism—all that is probably his most enduring myth of all, beating Major Tom, Ziggy Stardust and the rest of them hands down. If Berlin was genuinely a sanctuary after his mad years in the New World, it was no less a fantasy, something he himself understood well enough: "I thought I'd take the stage set, throw it away, and go and live in the real thing."

round and round

The next two songs, the Ballardian "Always Crashing in the Same Car" and "Be My Wife," signal a slight shift in form and mood. They both nod to a more conventional song structure, with "Be My Wife" even featuring a chorus of sorts. "Always Crashing" has a metal-ish guitar solo (albeit heavily treated), and even a proper end rather than a fade-out. Both have more of a narrative feel—elliptic and impressionistic though it might be. And both move into more self-aware, introspective territory, after the autism-from-the-inside of the preceding three tracks.

The rhythm bed of "Always Crashing in the Same Car" was laid down at the Château, but the song was one of the last to be completed at Hansa studios in Berlin in November 1976. "David spent quite a while writing the melody and lyrics," recounted Visconti in 2001, "and even recorded a verse in a quasi-Dylan voice. But it was too spooky (not

funny, as intended), so he asked me to erase it and we started again (in those days tracks were limited, since computers
and time sync codes, to latch two machines together, were
not in use yet)." The brief lyric was inspired by a real event.
One night, in the grip of paranoid psychosis, Bowie had
been cruising the streets in his Mercedes and had spotted a
dealer whom he was convinced had ripped him off. In a rage
he started ramming the dealer's car over and over again,
before finally driving off back to his hotel. There he found
himself maniacally driving around in circles in the hotel's
underground garage.

Bowie has said that Syd Barrett was an influence on "Be
My Wife," but the lyrics to "Always Crashing" also recall certain lines from Barrett's *Madcap Laughs*, an album that Bowie
has often praised, and has referenced before (the jokey,
skewed snatches of studio chatter on "Andy Warhol" from
Hunky Dory mimic those of "The Madcap Laughs").
Bowie's "I was going round and round the hotel garage,
must have been touching close to ninety-four" is pretty close
to Barrett's "You're spinning around and around in a car
with electric lights flashing very fast" (from "No Good
Trying"). Likewise, "Jasmine, I saw you peeping, as I put my
foot down to the floor" has something of Barrett's melancholy "Dark Globe" (a song Bowie has singled out as
Madcap's highlight): "Oh where are you now, pussy willow
that smiled on this leaf, when I was alone, you promised a
stone from your heart." (And there's also "singing through

the gloom," from the James Joyce poem "Golden Hair" that Barrett set to music on *Madcap*, which recalls Bowie's "talking through the gloom.")

Syd Barrett has been one of the touchstones of Bowie's artistic development. Seeing the charismatic Barrett perform with Pink Floyd at the Marquee in 1967 made Bowie realise what an English rock star could be—and of course Bowie went on to record Barrett's "See Emily Play" on *Pin-Ups*. There is a fair amount of Barrett in the Ziggy Stardust character (the Arnold Corns, the band Bowie initially formed to record the first Ziggy songs, was named after Barrett's song "Arnold Layne"). Before *Ziggy Stardust* there was *Hunky Dory*, which shows traces of Barrett's post-Floyd solo work in its whimsy and its acoustic, psych-folk feel. And the first side of *Low*, too, has something of Barrett's solo work about it. There's a similar attention deficiency, a slapdash feel; the songs—with their odd harmonic twists that musically don't quite cohere—stop seemingly halfway through as if the singer has suddenly lost interest. There's also the flat tone of the singing, the lyric mix of peculiar juxtapositions coupled with the occasional cliché, and the sudden mood swings and musical changes ("A New Career in a New Town"). Above all, there's the impression of seeing the schizophrenic mind from the inside, without too much awareness of the madness, and yet with introspective self-pity straining through every now and then, as it does on "Always Crashing in the

Same Car."*

It's a song about repeated failure transformed into recurring nightmare, with suicidal overtones. The image of crashing over and over again, and deliberately ("as I put my foot down to the floor"), recalls Iggy's "though I try to die you put me back on the line." The slower beat, Eno's swirling synth instrumentation and the ghostly keyboard treatments add to the track's oneiric feel. If "Always Crashing" doesn't feature the bedroom symbolism of the preceding three songs, the vision of a car tearing around a hotel garage nonetheless echoes the album's central image of enclosed spaces that both stifle and comfort. Instead of journeying from A to B, a car is turning around on itself, the only possible exit being into the deserts of the interior.

There's something Kraftwerkian and nostalgically retro about the theremin-like sounds Eno engineered on this track, recalling the futurism that synthesisers signalled in the popular culture of the fifties and sixties—in movie soundtracks like *The Forbidden Planet* (1956) for instance, or the theme tunes to "Star Trek" or "Doctor Who" (written in the

---

* Barrett has been an influence on Eno as well. Barrett's "Matilda Mother"—with its singularly enunciated singing style and its synth drones—seems to me to be something of a template for Eno's early solo work. At the time of making *Low*, Eno actually owned the Farfisa organ used on that Barrett track; a Farfisa is also used on *Low*, although I'm not sure whether it's the same one.

early sixties with an ancestor of the EMS synth Eno used on *Low*). In sixties pop, synths were used to sometimes gimmicky effect during the psychedelic years of 1966–67; they were then largely co-opted by prog rock groups in the early seventies, where a noodling synth sound often represented not so much machine futurism but fantasies of expanding consciousness and other suspect hippie notions. By the time of 1976's punk revolution, however, "electronic stuff was considered something you couldn't touch," explains one-time Ultravox! frontman John Foxx, who was also working with Eno at the time and moving in similar directions to Bowie and Kraftwerk. "It was too close to Pink Floyd, forbidden by Johnny Lydon, declared ungood."

By Bowie's own admission, punk "was virtually over by the time it lodged itself in my awareness." In a way, Bowie managed to wrongfoot the zeitgeist by not even being aware of it, instead channelling the themes and strategies that would become familiar in the post-punk era of the late seventies and early eighties. *Low*'s turn away from American to European romanticism, its focus on alienated subjectivities, on the artificial and the urban, its mix of modernist imagery and postmodern pastiche, its forefronting of a synthetic sound—these were all trademarks picked up in part or in toto by post-punk bands like Joy Division, Ultravox!, the Human League or American acts like Talking Heads and Devo.

sometimes you get nowhere

There's a sonic link between "Be My Wife" and the *Station to Station* album in its knees-up pub piano style that is also used on "TVC-15" (*Station*'s fourth track). "Be My Wife" is about as conventional as it gets on *Low*, and was the second single taken from the album. It has a verse and chorus and sticks to fairly straightforward band instrumentation. Essentially, though, it's still another mixed-up pastiche, coupling an English pub singalong feel with Dennis Davis's aggressive drum crash, a kitsch organ drone, lyrics that are too straightforward to be taken at face value, and Bowie's camped-up cockney accent that recalls his Newley-esque days as a would-be light entertainer. Britpop bands like Blur and Pulp clearly owe a debt to this song, and in turn, as Bowie remarked recently, " 'Be My Wife' owes a lot to Syd Barrett, actually." Certainly, Barrett's ability to integrate English whimsy and vaudeville into a rock format finds an echo here, and that Englishness underlines the fact that *Low* is very much Bowie's post-American album.

The lyric is the most straightforward of the album, and takes up *Station to Station*'s theme of restless travel as spiritual metaphor: "I've lived all over the world, I've left every place." But its dumb simplicity is something of a tease. "Please be mine, share my life, stay with me, be my wife…" Could this be anything but irony? The fact is that Bowie's marriage at this stage was in the final stages of disintegration. He would only see his wife a handful of times more, and would soon set about gaining legal custody of his son through the courts. So it was a rather strange refrain to be singing. And yet…the song isn't exactly ironic either. At least a part of the "sincerity" is sincere, and the passivity of its plea—asking for something but offering nothing—is of a piece with the rest of the album's lyrics. The song ends poignantly with the first line of a verse that is never completed. "It was genuinely anguished, I think," Bowie once said of the song, before adding: "It could have been anybody, though." That ambivalence strikes pretty much at the heart of not only the song and the first side of *Low*, but almost everything else Bowie did in the seventies. He'd always located himself in that interesting space where even the singer doesn't quite know what to make of his material. Is Bowie's *Young Americans* a straightforward celebration of Philly soul, or a tricksy postmodern appropriation of it? Surely a bit of both. (Eno has said of Bowie's 1992 marriage ceremony in Florence that "you couldn't tell what was sincere and what was theatre. It was very touching.")

"Be My Wife" was released as a single in June 1977, but unlike "Sound and Vision" it failed to make a dent in the charts on either side of the Atlantic. Bowie did, however, bother to make a video for it, directed by Stanley Dorfman, and it's undoubtedly one of his best efforts. A heavily made-up Bowie self-consciously hams it up with an unplugged guitar, illustrating the track's ambivalences with unsettling aplomb. "I think what's really unusual about it is the half-heartedness, the clumsiness," says writer and recording artist Momus (aka Nick Currie). "It's basically a rock video featuring a Pierrot act, a mime sketch of a rock star making a rock video, yet too comically glum and sulky to go through the required hoops, and lacking the necessary gung ho conviction. Ninety-nine percent of rock videos have full-throttle conviction, conviction turned up to 11. But here Bowie mimes a desultory half-heartedness with deft physical theatre. The character (because it isn't really Bowie, it's a fellow, a sad sack, a thin-lipped melancholic) makes to play his guitar and gives up half way through the phrase. He just can't be bothered. He's awkward, but the awkwardness is performed very gracefully. There's something of Buster Keaton in the performance, the grace with which clumsiness is evoked. (Keaton gets a little homage in a much later Bowie video, 'Miracle Goodnight.')"

moving on

Two instrumentals, "Speed of Life" and "A New Career in a New Town," bookend the first side—although they are somehow more songs without words than real instrumentals. "A New Career in a New Town" has no words apart from the unspoken title, and yet it conjures up perfectly the feeling of moving to a new town alone, with the mix of anxiety, solitude, nervous anticipation, forced optimism and the sense of looking forwards and back at the same time. The track was recorded at the Château, but the title no doubt came later, after Bowie's move to Berlin.

The track starts with a brief, fragile electronic passage, reminiscent of the textural interludes on *Radio-Activity*, although a touch more off-kilter than that. A smothered bass drum taps out a delicate beat that has an interestingly proto-House feel. It contrasts wildly with the crashing snare that comes in abruptly at 0:36 with the entirely different second theme, accompanied by Bowie's blues harmonica, and another bar-room melody in a "Be My Wife" mode, plonked out on treated keyboards. Again there is no bridge to return us to the initial Kraftwerkian fragment, which kicks in abruptly again at 1:22, before returning us again to the blues/honky-tonk of the second theme again at 1:36. Just as "Speed of Life" sets down a musical agenda of instruments fighting it out, "A New Career" takes it to an extreme, literally splicing together two fragments that seem to be not only two quite different bits of music but in two altogether different genres as well. Ultimately, it works, with both parts yearning towards something in their different ways.

The track is really the sonic equivalent of a Burroughs cut-up, juxtaposing clean-lined electronica with old-fashioned piano and harmonica to reflect that feeling of arriving and departing all at the same time. I'm intrigued as to how such experimentalist techniques often work better when transposed to popular culture, necessarily years and decades and eras after they were first deployed in the avant-garde of high modernism. Burroughs's cut-up method, as he applied it, is philosophically engaging but doesn't make for great reading (arguably, his best efforts are his more conventional autobiographical works, *Junky* and *Queer*). Perhaps something similar could be said about Stockhausen's electronics or Cage's tape loops. But modernist ideas, by now very second-hand, when appropriated by people like Bowie or Eno, can result in work that is just as culturally vital or even more so. Lazarus-like, modernism seemed to inject itself into popular culture years after its demise in the high cultures of art, literature and music. In a way, popular music as it developed in the fifties and sixties turns the cultural paradigm on its head. With pop, postmodernism always came before modernism. Pop culture didn't actually need an Andy Warhol to make it postmodern. Rock 'n' roll was never anything but a faked-up blues—something that the glam-era Bowie had understood perfectly. (Eno: "Some people say Bowie is all surface style and second-hand ideas, but that sounds like a definition of pop to me.")

honky château

Sessions at the Château d'Hérouville didn't go smoothly.
Most of the staff were on holiday, and the service was bad.
"After three days I noticed that the sound got duller and
duller," recalled Visconti, "and I asked my assistant, a love-
ly English chap, when was the last time the multitrack
recorder was lined up? He said about a week before we
arrived, then the technician went on holiday. My assistant
was brand new, hired just for us because he could speak
English and French. He didn't know how to maintain the
machines. So every morning I'd go into the control room
with him and we'd line up the machine together, with the
manual open, hoping for the best."

Food seemed to be another problem—hardly a help
given Bowie's obsessions about food poisoning. There was a
skeleton staff, and for the first few days there was little else
to eat apart from rabbit and no vegetables. When the musi-

cians complained, six lettuce heads were plonked down on the table, with oil and vinegar, and with more rabbit. Visconti again: "A French woman was hired to be our assistant. She was supposed to provide us with anything we might need to make the recording go smoothly, but even she couldn't be bothered to bring some bread, cheese and wine up to the studio when we called down for some at 1 a.m. (a normal working hour for a rock studio). I remember David getting the owner out of bed at that hour and saying in precise, measured out words, 'We want some bread, some cheese and some wine in the studio. Now! What, you're asleep? Excuse me, but I thought you were running a studio.'" Eventually, Bowie and Visconti came down with diarrhoea, precipitating the move to Berlin's Hansa studios to finish the album.

Bowie and Visconti got it into their heads that the Château was haunted. Bowie refused a master bedroom, since "it felt impossibly cold in certain areas of it," and had a dark corner near a window that seemed to suck light into it. Visconti took the room, which "felt like it was haunted as all fuck." Even Eno (a cooler head, one might imagine), supposedly claimed that he was woken early every morning by someone shaking his shoulder, except that when he opened his eyes there was no one there. Spooky castle clichés and Bowie's supernatural obsessions were clearly having their effect on the rest of the crew as well.

Bowie was not in good shape. He may have been "struggling to get well," but it was early days yet. Quite apart from the drug-induced mental health problems, he was also breaking up with his wife and fighting his former manager, Michael Lippman, in court. Visconti: "There were very rare periods when he was up and excited. Those moments were definitely captured on tape and he would go in and do a backing track, but this would be followed by long periods of depression." There were ugly scenes as well when Roy Martin, a former friend and now a lover of Angie's, turned up, resulting in a punch-up in the dining room, with Visconti having to separate the two men. It didn't take much for Bowie's paranoia to kick in: "He even grew a bit suspicious of me at one point," Visconti recalled, "although he had no cause to because I was one of the people who was keeping him sane on that album, and as a result got very close to him. I was with him night and day just trying to keep his head above water because he was really sinking—he was so depressed."

In the middle of the sessions, Bowie took time out to attend court proceedings in Paris against Michael Lippman, returning in a comatose state, pale and unable to work for several days. Eno: "He was pretty much living at the edge of his nervous system, very tense. But as often happens, that translated into a sense of complete abandon in the work. One of the things that happens when you're going through traumatic life situations is your work becomes one of the only places where you can escape and take control. I think it's in that sense that 'tortured' souls sometimes produce great work."

And that seemed to be the case with *Low*. However bad the external situation seemed to be, the work still materialised. Visconti: "It wasn't a difficult album to make, we were freewheeling, making our own rules." The Château itself had "no bearing on the form of the tonality of the work," according to Bowie, but he found the studio a joy to work in, with its ramshackle, lived-in feeling. And despite all the outside pressures, Bowie, Visconti and Eno were working well as a team. Interviewed at the time, guitarist Ricky Gardiner also enthused about the project: "The sessions are going really well. I had a surprising amount of freedom. I'd ask what kind of things he wanted, for instance, and we'd have a vague discussion about it for two or three minutes. Whatever I did seemed to fit, and that went for all the other musicians."

city of ghosts

By the end of September, with most of the tracks down, Bowie left for Berlin, where the album would be finished and mixed. It was a move that had been brewing a long time, and Bowie would end up staying in the city for over two years. At first he took up residence in a suite in the Hotel Gehrus, in an old castle not far from the Grunewald forest, but soon moved to a 19th century residential block at 155 Hauptstrasse in the Schoneburg district, above a shop selling auto parts. While certainly a comedown from French and German castles, the building nonetheless had a shabby grandeur to it, with wrought-iron gates that led onto the street. Bowie's seven-room, first-floor apartment was in poor repair but recalled the discreet charms of another era's *haute bourgeoisie*, with its parquet floors, high ceilings, decorative cornices and panelled doors. There were rooms for Iggy Pop (although he would soon move to his own pad on the fourth floor), Corinne Schwab and Bowie's son and nanny (who had been with him at the Château as well). There was an office for Bowie, and an artist's studio as well—Bowie had taken to painting portraits that were of a rather derivative Expressionist style. In his bedroom, above the bed, hung his own portrait of Japanese novelist Yukio Mishima (1925–70), who spectacularly committed ritual suicide after a tragi-comic coup attempt (in other words, a very Bowie-esque character).

Bowie stopped dyeing his hair orange, grew a moustache and started wearing workingmen's overalls as a sort of disguise, although one of the pleasures of Berlin was that no one bothered him much anyway. He quickly got into a routine of staying in bed until the afternoon then brunching on coffee, orange juice and cigarettes before walking to Hansa, where he would often work through the night. Daytime pleasures, when he indulged in them, included idling in coffeehouses and riding around the wide spaces of the city on bikes with Iggy and Coco. "I just can't express the feeling of freedom I felt there," he told *Uncut* magazine in 2001. "Some days the three of us would jump into the car and drive like crazy through East Germany and head down to the Black Forest, stopping off at any small village that caught our eye. Just go for days at a time. Or we'd take long, all-afternoon lunches at the Wannsee on winter days. The place had a glass roof and was surrounded by trees and still exuded an atmosphere of the long gone Berlin of the twenties."

He often visited art galleries on both sides of the Wall, but his favourite was the Brücke museum in Dahlem in the Berlin suburbs, devoted to a group of artists who were working in Berlin and Dresden before the First World War. The Brücke ("Bridge") movement—which included artists such as Kirchner, Bleyl, Heckel and Nolde—developed an impressionistic style of painting that aimed not at any sort of realist reading of a subject, but rather an inner emotion. Landscapes are simplified to broad brush strokes, colours are abstracted until they break free of the object, which in turn becomes merely a vehicle to express the interior state. Just as the Cubists in France were inspired by the stripped-down and exaggerated nature of primitive art, the Brücke artists looked for inspiration in the thick lines and spare design of medieval woodcuts, to create a German version of the avant-garde scene in Paris. Although spiritual renewal was an overriding theme, the works themselves give off a sense of brooding anxiety and nostalgic melancholy; the portraits often have a strange distance to them, like haunted masks.

The Brücke artists (and Expressionism in general) were more than just passing fancies for Bowie; the interest had remained with him since art school. "When I was in Berlin I'd find old woodblock prints from the Brücke school, in small shops, at unbelievable prices, and to buy like that was wonderful." There's a clear philosophical link between their work and the inward turn of *Low*'s second side, the notion of landscape as emotion: "It was an art form that mirrored life not by event but by mood," Bowie said in 2001, "and this was where I felt my work was going."

At night, Bowie explored yet another peeling layer of the Berlin myth. The nightclub scene was a bizarre mix of the very new and the very old, a bit like the population of Berlin itself at the time—the middle generation having been swept away in the cataclysm of war. Iggy Pop's "Nightclubbing" gives a good enough flavour of what it was like to be out on the tiles with Bowie. The pair of them would frequent cabarets, and a transvestite bar where the velvet seats and smoky mirror had been preserved intact since before the war, as explained to Bowie by a 75-year old art dealer who'd been going there since the days of Marlene Dietrich in the 1920s. In Romy Haag's club, "her cabaret was on a stage about ten feet wide and she used to have as many as twenty people on that stage all doing these quick vignettes," recalls Visconti. "They'd put strobe lights on and then they'd mime to the records. I remember Romy herself did a great mime to one of David's records, "Amsterdam," but it was all speeded up so that the voice was in a female range. It was quite bizarre and you felt you were in a Fellini film." It was the Christopher Isherwood side of Berlin, which had Bowie fascinated during his initial months in the city. And photos of the time show Bowie very much acting the part of the Weimar-era Berliner, in his pinch-front fedora and leather overcoat.

On the other side of the age equation, Berlin was also full of young people, and especially artists, attracted to the city thanks to generous government grant schemes and a dispensation from national service. West Berlin had largely been cleared of industry due to its physical isolation, leaving behind huge warehouse spaces that artists and musicians would transform into studios, with government aid. It led to a vibrant alternative culture; musicians would be coming and going through Hansa studios and Bowie would be socialising with people like Tangerine Dream's Edgar Froese, with whom he shared a rehearsal stage built into an old theatre. Often enough, Bowie would "hang with the intellectuals and beats at the Exile restaurant in Kreutzberg. In the back they had this smoky room with a billiard table and it was sort of like another living room except the company was always changing."

But the early months were traumatic. He and Iggy had come to Berlin to "kick drugs in the heroin capital of the world," in the words of Iggy Pop—although thankfully heroin held little appeal. Bowie had cut back on his cocaine intake but hadn't killed the habit altogether; some mornings he'd still be locking himself in the bathroom. Other days he might knock back a bottle of whisky, "just to get rid of the depression." He was once spotted in a bar, alone and sobbing. And he was still suffering from paranoia, obsessed with the "leeches" who were bleeding him. He could fall into autistic detachment, refusing to look people in the eye, doodling and drawing as they tried to talk to him. "His job was to work, and his joy was in discussing it—if a mumbled yep or nope could be elevated to discussion," was how one colleague at Hansa put it.

Essentially, the less coke Bowie did, the more he drank. One waiter at a Kurfürstendamm beer house remembers him throwing up in the gutter after drinking a gallon of König-Pilseners. "Virtually every time I saw him in Berlin, he was drunk, or working on getting drunk," Angie Bowie wrote in her biography. She'd turn up in Berlin unexpectedly, throwing Bowie into a state of emotional turmoil. During one of those visits, an anxiety attack had Bowie thinking he had heart problems and he wound up spending the night in a hospital. "I couldn't understand why he'd gone to Berlin. He never asked me if I wanted to live there. It never once occurred to David to stay at home with Zowie and me. His boredom threshold was too intense to live with. He swung from genius to the erratic without warning." It all came to a dramatic head when, in a jealous rage, Angie demanded that Bowie fire his assistant, Corinne Schwab. When Bowie refused, Angie tried to burn Corinne's room, then slashed her clothes and threw them out onto the street along with the bed, and caught the next flight out of Berlin. Angie and Bowie would only meet one more time, to exchange legal documents relating to their divorce.

Berlin was an island, cut off from the world, but big enough to get lost in as well. Each layer of the Berlin myth seemed to reflect something in the Bowie persona—the Expressionist artists; the cabaret decadence; the Nazi megalomania; the cataclysmic destruction; the isolation behind the Wall; the Cold War depression; the ghosts who never depart. Above all, Berlin wasn't quite real. Its military zones, the bullet-holes still pockmarking the edifices, the watch-towers, Speer's megalithic relics, the bombed-out buildings next to shiny new ones, the huge black tanks that rumbled along the streets…as Visconti put it, "You could have been on the set of *The Prisoner*."

do you remember that dream?

Low's second side represents a drastic mood change. The nervy, fragmented art-funk gives way to four longer, slower textural pieces that descend into mutism. Because Bowie deliberately divided *Low*'s tracks up in the way he did, rather than scatter these "ambient" pieces throughout the album, it's hard not to read off a structural metanarrative. On the one hand, the division reflects split mentalities; on the other, the second side becomes the logical consequence of the first. In that respect, the album bears some similarities to Joy Division's *Closer*, which is not a concept album, but one where the sequencing leads us somewhere ever darker as we progress. The jittery psychosis of *Low*'s first side describes a mindset that could have led somewhere equally suicidal (just as *The Idiot* signed off with the terminally morbid "Mass Production"). But although the second side's pieces are soaked in melancholy, they are neither suicidal nor entirely nihilistic. There's even something vaguely uplifting about the first three. They are, however, profoundly solipsistic. The autism and retreat of the first side's lyrics find their wordless counterpart here as the music lifts off and spins into inner orbit, free from external reference points. Like the landscapes of the Brücke artists, the four pieces superficially describe a place (Warsaw on the first track, Berlin on the other three), but that place is really just a prompt, just a vehicle for a mood. And in the case of "Warszawa," Bowie was only in Warsaw for a matter of hours, while changing trains. If this is a portrait of a city, as the title implies, it is painted with the broadest of brushstrokes.

"Warszawa" is the only piece on the album where Eno shares writing credits (although oddly he's also co-credited with "Art Decade" on the *Stage* live album). Its genesis is that Bowie simply told Eno he wanted a slow piece with a very emotive, almost religious feel to it. Eno suggested they begin by laying down a track with 430 metronome clicks (the same method was used for "Art Decade" and "Weeping Wall"). It gave them a sort of pulse to improvise over, rather than falling into a more conventional 3/4 or 4/4 time signature. It's a pulse that bears resemblances to the minimalist "groove" used by composers such as Philip Glass and Steve Reich. Once they had around seven minutes of clicks on tape, Visconti would then call out the click numbers on another track. That enabled them to construct the piece: there were no bars of music, just chords and sections coming in and overlapping at randomly picked click numbers, like at click 59 for instance. The technique gave the piece room to breathe, without the conventional constrictions of two-, four- or eight-bar phrasing. They used the Roland and Yamaha keyboards that were at hand at the Château studios, plus Eno's EMS synth and Bowie's chamberlain (a version of the tape-based mellotron sampling keyboard). A piano and guitar were also used, although they were heavily treated by Visconti.

Almost all the instrumental work was done by Eno alone while Visconti was accompanying Bowie to Paris, where he had to attend court hearings against his former manager. Eno: "Rather than wasting the studio time I decided to start a piece on my own, with the understanding that if he didn't like it I'd pay for the studio time and use it myself." Visconti's son Delaney had a hand in the proceedings as well. One afternoon, the four-year-old was sitting at the studio piano playing the notes A, B, C over and over again. Eno sat next to him and completed the melody which would become the "Warszawa" theme.

On Bowie's return from Paris, Eno played him what he'd come up with. "As soon as David heard it he said, 'Get me a mike,'" Eno recalled in 1995. "He's very fast when he gets going, really a brilliant singer—I don't think people realise how finely he can tune his singing, in terms of picking a particular emotional pitch: it's really scientific the way he does it, very interesting. He'll say, 'I think that's slightly too the-

atrical there, it should be more withdrawn and introspective'
—and he'll go in and sing it again, and you'll hear this point-
four of a degree shift which makes all the difference.... He
picks up the mood of a musical landscape, such as the type
I might make, and he can really bring it to a sharp focus,
both with the words he uses and the style of singing he
chooses."

Bowie came up with the words in about ten minutes,
according to Visconti. He had a record with him of a Balkan
boys' choir that he liked, and he wanted to do something
with the same feeling. Visconti slowed down the tape by two
semitones for Bowie to sing the high-pitched part, so that
when played back normally he sounded like a young choir
boy. The words are in a made-up language that sounds
vaguely Eastern European, vaguely ethnic, and very atmospheric, as though from both the distant past and the distant
future. There's perhaps a connection with Dadaist sound
poetry, and its links to Primitivism and Expressionism (Eno
would sample sound poet Kurt Schwitters on "Before and
after Science" the following year). In any case, doing away
with the semantic on this track and on "Subterraneans" is a
masterstroke, giving these songs the eerie sense of watching
a movie in a foreign language, where you can feel all the different moods without understanding the plot. It follows the
Expressionist principle, where the object painted might
almost be anything, as the colours and brushstrokes obliter-
ate it to reflect the inner state. The "nothing to say" of

"Sound and Vision" finds its true expression and meaning on the second side of *Low*.

"Warszawa" is a slow, tolling piece that reminds me a little of Estonian composer Arvo Pärt's mournful "Cantus in Memory of Benjamin Britten" (1977). It starts with bare octaves in A, followed by a modal melody also in octaves, then modulates to D-sharp minor in the main section of the piece. Bowie's heartfelt, nonsense singing doesn't come in until well over halfway through, at 4:05, before giving way to the main theme again. The piece doesn't fade out, but it doesn't have an ending either, it just stops in its tracks at some point. Despite this, and the planned randomness of its construction, a sense of deep structure does eventually emerge from the track. Some critics have written off the second side of *Low* as Eno's work, but I think the careful structuring of this track and its harmonies actually show something of a Bowie influence on Eno, whose own ambient pieces tend to be less compositional, less interested in harmony, and in general less teleological.

"Warszawa's" introductory piano drone bears more than a passing resemblance to the intro of Scott Walker's mesmerising, psycho-sexual meditation on torture, "The Electrician," recorded the following year (and described by Bowie as "one of the most astonishing performances in popular music"). Scott Walker is another Bowie touchstone, and, like Kraftwerk, another of those artists whose careers seem to intertwine with Bowie's. Back in the sixties, Bowie had already heard Walker's existential solo albums, and more particularly his versions of Jacques Brel songs. Bowie's own Brel recordings ("My Death" and "Amsterdam") were much more Walker than Brel, and used the same loose translations by Mort Schuman. Walker's career floundered for most of the seventies but in 1977 he wrote and sang four songs on the Walker Brothers album *Nite Flights* that move into very similar territory to Bowie's *Low* and *"Heroes"*, mixing funk /disco beats with dissonant synths, scratchy guitar and fragmented lyrics of a modernist bent ("The Electrician" is a sort of update of Joseph Conrad's Mr Kurtz). Walker had heard *Low* before embarking on his own darkly experimental tracks, and he sent Bowie a copy of *Nite Flights* on its release in early 1978, despite the fact that the two had never met. Bowie was enthused; a couple of years later he offered Walker his services as a producer, but it seems Walker turned him down (he later went into the studios with Eno, but ultimately nothing came of that project). Much later, Bowie recorded his own version of "Nite Flights" on *Black Tie White Noise* (1993). More recently, he has talked up Scott Walker's operatic *Tilt* (1995)—a late, fascinating entry into the modernist canon.

all that fall

"Art Decade" was started at the Château but completed at Hansa studios. Bowie has said that it is about West Berlin, "a city cut off from its world, art and culture, dying with no hope of retribution." Actually it doesn't sound as depressed as that, although instrumentally and texturally it does leave that impression of a world caught just before it disappears, with the constant descent of the main theme and the odd, almost organic-sounding electronic effects that drop pitch then fade. The title puns on "decayed" but also evokes "art deco," and the sense of nostalgia for the elegant innocence of an age just before the cataclysm of the trenches. A cello part, scored by Visconti and played by the album's sound engineer Eduard Meyer, adds warmth to this luminous track that recalls the work of Harmonia and the early, more pastoral Kraftwerk.

According to Eno, "Art Decade" "started off as a little

tune [Bowie] played on the piano. Actually we both played it because it was for four hands, and when we'd finished it he didn't like it very much and sort of forgot about it. But as it happened, during the two days he was gone I finished the one piece ['Warszawa'] and then dug that out to see if I could do anything with it. I put all those instruments on top of what we had, and then he liked it and realised there was hope for it, and he worked on top of that, adding more instruments. In fact, 'Art Decade' is my favourite track of all." The piece starts off with an enigmatic, muffled intro that sounds like it's coming from somewhere very far away. The main modal motif makes an abrupt entrance, is repeated several times, and then is freeze-framed on a four-note figure, mesmerically repeated over and over again, as though a fade-out was imminent, although it's not.

That endless repetition with very slight changes is reminiscent of minimalist composer Philip Glass, and minimalism's foregrounding of repetition and texture over melodic complication. Indeed, *Low*'s whole second side shows a minimalist influence, which was already apparent on *Station to Station* (not just in the title track but also in the taut repetitions of "Golden Years"). And Glass is yet another of those artists with whom Bowie has had intertwining musical relations. Bowie had seen Glass's *Music for Changing Parts* in 1971, and the two had met not long after and became friendly. At the time of making *Low*, Bowie was certainly listening to Glass—and vice versa, as Glass himself testifies: "I remember talking to David at the time and was impressed to hear that *Low* was meant to be part of a trilogy. I'd never encountered pop music conceived with that level of artistic ambition. I thought at the time I'd like to do something with that material, but didn't carry the thought any further." Although the gestation period was long, he did eventually carry it further. His *Low Symphony*, based on three pieces from the album ("Subterraneans," "Some Are" [a *Low* outtake] and "Warszawa"), was written in the spring of 1992 and came out in 1993. Personally, I find what Glass did with *Low* a disappointment, and I say that as a fan of Glass's work. He essentially takes Bowie's and Eno's melody lines, "Glassifies" them and orchestrates them in a pretty conventional fashion. Glass seems to miss the point that what makes *Low* interesting is its studio-based nature. In this case, you can't successfully divorce the music from the processes that made it, because by doing that you take out the most distinctive ingredient. Nonetheless, the experiment underlines the bootstrapping relationship between pop and minimalism. Because although minimalism is a clear influence on *Low*, popular music itself had a strong influence on minimalism. The minimalist "groove" is classical music's equivalent of a pop beat, and the repetitions and simplified melodic structures also recall the strictures of the three-minute single of the late fifties or early sixties.

"Art Decade's" "freeze-framed" repetitions aren't resolved but work themselves up into a slow-burning, restrained climax, before unexpectedly giving way to the main theme again, cutting directly in to the four-note figure. Bowie and Eno used the metronome click technique on this track as well, and the randomness of the sequence changes works to good effect. That jolt of the return is almost the opposite of what Eno achieved on the ambient pieces of *Another Green World*, and is in fact rather at odds with the whole notion of "ambient" music. And the reappearance of the main theme brings the piece to a close with a certain symmetry that is again more the compositional mark of Bowie than Eno.

pulsations

The shimmering "Weeping Wall" is the only piece on the album that was entirely recorded in Berlin. And it is of course "about the Berlin Wall—the misery of it," although the title also echoes Jerusalem's Wailing Wall, with its similar connotations of exile and lamentation. It's an all-Bowie affair—he plays every instrument on the track, and Eno has said he had nothing to do with its creation.

It's also the track that is most marked by minimalism—to the extent that it could almost pass as a Steve Reich composition. It bears a lot of similarities with the pulse sections of Reich's seminal "Music for 18 Musicians." I was very surprised to learn that the Reich work wasn't released on record by ECM until 1978, well after *Low*, but a little research reveals that it had its European première in Berlin, in October 1976—in other words the same month Bowie was making "Weeping Wall." Reich confirms that Bowie was at that concert. Sometimes credited as the progenitor of sampling, Reich is a good illustration of the way minimalism and popular music have mutually enriched one another. From a 1999 interview: "Cut to 1974, and my ensemble is giving a concert in London, and when the concert's over a young man with long hair comes up and looks at me and says, 'How do you do, I'm Brian Eno.' Two years later we're in Berlin and David Bowie's there, and I think to myself, 'This is great, this is poetic justice.' I'm the kid sitting at the bar listening to Miles Davis, listening to John Coltrane, and now these people are listening to me!"

The Reich piece and "Weeping Wall" share a similar sonic quality thanks to the mix of wordless chanting, xylophones and particularly a vibraphone that Bowie found abandoned at the Hansa studio (it's a type of marimbaphone that creates a special vibrato, invented by Herman Winterhoff in 1916). The effect has the flavour of Javanese gamelan (traditional Indonesian orchestras that use a similar instrument to the vibraphone) and adds to the generic "ethnic" feel of the second side, initiated with Bowie's faux-Eastern wailings on "Warszawa." Both "Weeping Wall" and "Music for 18 Musicians" privilege a sort of pulsation rather than a more conventional rhythm, aiming at a certain "stillness in motion." Reich's interest at this stage was in harmony and tonal quality rather than melodic construction—mirroring Bowie's and Eno's own textural leanings at the time. There is little sign of melody in the Reich pulse pieces, just a series of slight harmonic changes that occur at certain intervals, often just inversions of minor to major chords or vice versa. But there is a brief melody line on "Weeping Wall," although it's of secondary importance to the pulse and texture of the instrumentation. It's played at first on Bowie's ARP then repeated with variations vocally as a chant. Actually, it's the first few notes of "Scarborough Fair" repeated over and over. The borrowing may well be unintentional, but it does add a certain pastoral mysticism to the track.

Where "Weeping Wall" veers away from Reich is its playing of organic sounds (percussive instruments, vocals) off the harsher synthetic ones—one of *Low*'s key musical strategies. With the backing track of bubbling xylophone and vibraphone sounds down, Bowie once again used the metronome click method to randomly introduce chants and hums, synths and a distorted guitar riff to give the piece a distinctive flavour. Although there's a sense of mysterious yearning to the track, there's also a playful lightness and energy in there. It has a distance to it but doesn't feel particularly depressive to me, and its connection with the miseries of the Berlin Wall aren't overly apparent. In keeping with the other tracks of this side, though, you can't really escape its inwardness, and the feeling of listening to the soundtrack of images forever locked inside someone else's brain. And like just about every other track on the album, it has no real ending, but simply fades out at a seemingly random moment.

afterlife

A quick word on the afterlife of the album, before we move on to the last track. The mixing of *Low* was completed at Hansa-by-the-wall on November 16, 1976. Bowie's record company, RCA, had initially intended to get it out for Christmas, but when they heard the finished product they were taken aback by its lack of commercial potential, and delayed release. One executive at RCA apparently said he would personally buy Bowie a house in Philadelphia so that he could write and record *Young Americans II*. Even Tony DeFries, a former manager with whom Bowie had long since parted company, but who retained a sales percentage, briefly returned to the scene. Visconti: "Tony DeFries suddenly arrived and still purported to be David's manager. RCA complained that there weren't enough vocals…David just looked at the small print of the contract which read that they had to put it out." The album was eventually released in mid-January 1977, a week after Bowie's thirtieth birthday. In the face of RCA's reservations, and despite the fact that Bowie refused to be interviewed for its release or do any promotion, *Low* was still no kind of commercial failure, reaching number 2 in the UK charts and number 11 in the States.

The record sleeve features a heavily treated still from *The Man Who Fell to Earth*, already used for a paperback reissue of the original Walter Travis novel, and designed by Bowie's old school friend George Underwood. *The Man Who Fell to Earth* had by then come and gone in the movie theatres, so the sleeve choice wasn't a question of promoting the film, and points to the connection Bowie made between film and album. *Station to Station* had already featured a still from the film—a modish black-and-white image of a sleekly dressed Thomas Jerome Newton stepping into his spaceship. The image on *Low* is quite different, with a blank-faced Bowie in mugshot profile (title and image combine to make the "low profile" pun), wearing a less than stylish English duffel-coat. The dominant colour is an autumnal orange. Bowie's hair is exactly the same shade as the swirling, Turner-esque background, underlining the solipsistic notion of place reflecting person, object and subject melding into one.

Bowie biographies tend to say that *Low* got bad press on release, which may be true in the States, but a glance at the UK music papers of the week of January 22, 1977, reveals reviews that are in general far more positive than negative, although critics were rather confounded by Bowie's new direction. The reviews were filled with gloomy mid-seventies sociological riffs that bear no great relevance to *Low*, but nonetheless reflect the album's alienation. "Conceptually we are picking up where *Station to Station* left off: the western world's enslavement to time and consequent devaluation of place," the *NME* informs us. "*Low* is the ONLY contemporary rock album," and side two is "stunningly beautiful if you can get past taking it as some kind of personal insult." Over at *Sounds*, Tim Lott declared that "*Low* is the most difficult piece of music Bowie has ever put his name to." The listener has to work hard but "in the last word, it works, though on an unusual half-hidden level." For *Melody Maker*, *Low* is "oddly the music of Now—not exactly currently popular, but what seems right for the times. Bowie is brilliant in his dissection of mass communication."

In any case, it wasn't long after *Low*'s release before it was realised that the album was a milestone, both as an exemplary work in itself, and in the development of popular music. A whole strand of post-punk owes its existence to some sort of combination of the glam-era and Berlin-era Bowie personae; to Bowie's and Eno's injection of the synthetic into the three-minute pop song; to Visconti's and Dennis Davis's aggressive drum thrash; to the album's funk/electronic hybrid; to the turn towards a European aesthetic; to the non-pop experimentalism of the second side; to *Low*'s appropriation of modernist alienation. Even as late as 2000, Radiohead was attempting certain similar things with *Kid A* (the instrumental track on that album, "Treefingers," could almost have been on *Low*).

Since its release, *Low*'s critical stock has kept rising, and the album, in one way or another, has continued to live its life and even further evolve. Bowie's 1978 release *Stage* featured a number of live versions of *Low* songs; and the 1991 Ryko *Low* reissue included three extra tracks—a forgettable remix of "Sound and Vision" plus two outtakes from the original *Low* sessions, both credited to Bowie/Eno. "All Saints" is a plodding synthesiser instrumental that is interesting enough, but doesn't really go anywhere and ultimately sounds derivative of German synth bands like Cluster. But "Some Are" is a gem: a fragile, atmospheric piece with wintry images, a faint ghostly choir in the background and strange half-organic noises, exuding the same sort of quietude as "Art Decade." It could have happily sat somewhere on side two of the album; my guess is that it was dropped because its tolling piano intro is a little too similar to that of "Warszawa." In 1992, Philip Glass premiered his *Low* symphony; and in 2002 Bowie performed *Low* in its entirety as part of his curatorship of London's Meltdown Festival. Bowie's albums are gradually being re-released in thirtieth-anniversary double-CD reissues with bonus tracks, so perhaps we can expect further *Low* material to be unearthed for 2007. (One recent biography refers to "dozens of bittersweet songs" recorded during the *Low* sessions but not released because Bowie wanted a harder sound. The unreleased *The Man Who Fell to Earth* soundtrack might be another candidate, since Paul Buckmaster apparently still has the recordings on DAT in his archive.)

homesick blues

Low's final track—and for me *Low*'s most moving moment —was also the first to be conceived, since it was built over a piece from those *Man Who Fell to Earth* sessions of late 1975. "Subterraneans" is ostensibly about "the people who got caught in East Berlin after the separation—hence the faint jazz saxophones representing the memory of what it was." It's a sombre, hermetic piece featuring a slow, five-note bass figure that repeats itself at intervals throughout the track. On top of this, Bowie layers on even slower synth lines and also disorientating backwards tape sounds —something he'd already used to good effect on the intro to "Sweet Thing" on *Diamond Dogs*, and would use again on "Move On" (*Lodger*). There is a melancholy wordless chant, and then at 3:09 comes a beautifully emotive saxophone line (a very Bowie-esque touch). It's played by Bowie himself in the mournful Dorian mode, and has an improvised jazz feeling. There's an ache to it that could indeed reflect the plight of East Berliners trapped behind the Wall, but is really just an abstraction of that universal sense of the sorrow of vanished things.

With its film soundtrack genesis, the track could just as easily be the mindscape of Thomas Jerome Newton as he remembers a lost family and home in an alien world. Given the title, "Subterraneans" makes one think of a dark underworld, a civilisation forced underground in the aftermath of some great cataclysm. In fact, for me it recalls Chris Marker's enigmatic short film *La Jetée* (1962). That film is "the story of a man marked by an image from his childhood," and uses voice-over and expressionistic black-and-white still photography to evoke a subterranean world following nuclear catastrophe, exploring all those themes of memory, loss, dream, fate and the ever-present ghosts that "Subterraneans" also seems to evoke. (*La Jetée* later inspired the video for Bowie's "Jump They Say," the 1993 track he wrote about his schizophrenic half-brother, Terry.)

At 3:51 (again well over halfway through the track—the words are so often late to the scene on this album), we get the nonsense lyric: "share bride failing star, care-line, care-line, care-line, care-line, briding me shelley, shelley umm" (or something to that effect). It's half Kurt Schwitters, half Lewis Carroll. It doesn't mean anything (unless failing star is a reference to *The Man Who Fell to Earth*), but is extraordinarily affecting nonetheless—as if Bowie is desperately scrabbling to interpret the final thoughts of some dying world before it's too late. It is a more extreme breakdown of communication than the imaginary Eastern language of "Warszawa," because there are English words in there that we recognise, but still it doesn't cohere into anything grammatical or semantic. We've gone beyond that, to the point where the words are reconfigured into a completely private language, as the ultimate act of autism.

Language—the deflection of it, the refusal of it, the stripping it of sense, the attempt to get past it—is a key concern of the album. The three-letter *Low* is already a radically minimal title, and the lyric sheet to *Low* has only 410 words, barely a paragraph's worth (compared with well over 2,000 for *Diamond Dogs*). The refusal of language is also the refusal of narrative, another of Bowie's preoccupations on *Low:* "Eno got me off narrative," he said at the time. "Brian really opened my eyes to the idea of processing, to the abstract of the journey of the artist." Telling stories was something that English popular music had always done, had continued to do into the pop era with the Beatles, the Kinks, the Stones, then on to Bowie, with his quasi-concept albums of the early seventies and the skewed vignettes of songs like "Panic in Detroit" or "Young Americans." On the other hand, a lot of the German experimental music of the time had turned away from the narrative impulse, except maybe in an abstract structural sense. An album like Can's *Tago Mago* does something similar to *Low*, with its funk experimentalism of the first half giving way to the disturbed inner space of the second half, where not only words but music itself is more or less jettisoned in favour of textural sound. Implicit in the rejection of narrative is the rejection of a certain Romantic tradition.

crash your plane, walk away

"Subterraneans," and *Low* itself, ends in an impasse. After Bowie's emotional nonsense incantation, the Gregorian-style chant returns, and so does the saxophone, making a final subdued, tentative stab at some sort of melodic line before the edifice crumbles, again seemingly mid-track. We're refused the dramatic finale Bowie had given us on previous albums. There are no rock 'n' roll suicides, histrionic torch songs, dystopian hysterics, *femmes fatales* who will be your living end.

It strikes me that the nonsense lyric of "Subterraneans" has something of the childlike about it, of a small child struggling to explain the inexplicable with a confusion of words he doesn't yet understand. Against the backdrop of the imaginary languages, hums, chants and vocal wordlessness of the second side, those first-side images of bedroom refuge now start to clarify, start to feel like a psychoanalytic return. We leave *Low* with the feeling that the journey we've made is a mapless, backwards one, to the blind, pre-lingual world that will remain forever mysterious.

Paris, May 2005

bibliography

Books

Bowie, Angie, *Backstage Passes*, Cooper Square Press, 2000

Buckley, David, *Strange Fascination*, Virgin Publishing, 2001

Gillman, Peter and Leni Gillman, *Alias David Bowie, a Biography*, Henry Holt & Co, 1987

Juby, Kerry, *In Other Words*, Omnibus Press, 1986

Pegg, Nicholas, *The Complete David Bowie*, Reynolds & Hearn, 2004

Power, David, *David Bowie: A Sense of Art*, Pauper's Press, 2003

Sandford, Christopher, *Bowie: Loving the Alien*, Da Capo Press, 1998

Tremlett, George, *David Bowie: Living on the Brink*, Carroll & Graf Publishers, 1997

Thompson, Dave, *David Bowie: Moonage Daydream*, Plexus Publishing, 1994

Thomson, Elizabeth and David Gutman, eds., *The Bowie Companion*, 1996

Websites

http://www.algonet.se/~bassman
http://members.ol.com.au/rgriffin/goldenyears
http://www.tonyvisconti.com
http://www.menofmusic.com
http://www.teenagewildlife.com
http://www.bowiewonderworld.com

A note on references:

Some of the direct quotes from Bowie, Eno, Visconti et al. are from the works listed in the above bibliography, in particular those by David Buckley and Kerry Juby. However, most come from a wide range of articles published in the music press over the past 25 years. Quotes from Laurent Thibault are my translations from "Mémoires d'un Idiot" by Christophe Geudin, *Recording Musicien*, March 2002. For specific references for all other quotes, please contact me at hugowilcken@hotmail.com.

Also available in the series